A GOD STORY

**For those who believe in miracles.
And for those who need to.**

Lynn Kennedy

What readers are saying about this book:

ലഇ ฉൈ

"When you read this book **you'll never wonder again if God really knows** what we need before we ask. So don't rush it...this is one that will give you a story in the morning that will cause you to bask all day in the joyous ways God provides answers."

- Mrs. Marcia McKinney: conference leader, teacher, pastor's wife

"**Reading and digesting this book will warm your heart and bless your soul.**"

- Samuel E. Molind, DMD, Director of Global Health Outreach

"I have known Lynn for over 20 years. One thing that has been blazingly evident throughout those years is her passion for her Lord and her passion to bring the lost into relationship with her Lord......now, for the first time, Lynn has **beautifully put into writing just a few 'God Stories'** for your benefit and for mine. So, take the book, hunker down somewhere (don't forget the coffee!!) and enjoy reading what Abba, Father has done and then dream of what He can do ... through you!

- Marilyn Mallory, Director of Family Care, Edgewood Children's Ranch

"As I was reading this book I was deeply moved by the Savior's love for His own. To read of the modern-day miracles and the amazing detail God brings about to accomplish His plans and purposes was a thrill to my soul. I have experienced miracles in my own life and this **fresh reminder of His power and His love** make my memories even sweeter. This book has brought joyous praise to my heart for my great God and King of all."
- Mrs. Shirley Gibbs, Pastor's wife

ACKNOWLEDGEMENTS

൭൭ ൭൭

This book could never have been written if there had been no story to tell! I thank our God for the work He is doing in Burkina Faso, West Africa and beyond! I thank Him for saving and calling out many Dagara believers as evangelists, pastors, teachers, church planters, worship leaders and children's workers.

I wish to thank all of our Shattering Darkness *FAITH PARTNERS,* individuals and churches, *(you know who you are).* Your selfless giving enables us to obey the call of the Savior upon our lives. It excites me and honors our Lord Jesus to witness partnerships including Baptist churches, Presbyterian churches, Congregational churches, Nazarene churches, Lutheran and Methodist churches as well as interdenominational ministries joining as one to proclaim the Savior and His salvation to the peoples of West Africa!

Many thanks to Jamie, Karen, Linda, Chris, Doc and Dr. Tim, only our Lord will be able to repay you for your time, prayers, generosity and trust.

Thanks also are extended to Dr. David Uth, Reverend Bill Mitchell and the Global Impact Missions staff of First Baptist Church Orlando, my home church.

A special thank you to the many churches bringing IMPACT teams to West Africa so that many tribes and nations are now hearing of our Glorious Savior!

Thank you Marilyn, Shirley, Marcia, Nancy and Dr. Sam Molind for your input, editing and corrections!

Thank You, Lord Jesus, for my earthly family. Deb and Tom, Amy and Bri, I thank you for loving me. Patrice and Celine, thank you for loving and obeying our Jesus, no matter the cost. Narcisse, Rosie and Elisee.....Grandma loves you beyond measure!

TABLE OF CONTENTS

ᢓᐞ ᢓᐞ

DEDICATION

⌒ﲬ ﲬ⌒

To the One Who waited 29 years for me! The greatest Miracle Worker of all! So to my Savior, my King and my Lord: "I hank You, Beloved Jesus for not giving up on me. Thank You for taking me by the hand and teaching me all about Your love and forgiveness, second chances and fresh starts. Thank You for Your living word, Your Holy Spirit, Your beloved Name and Your Miracle performing power!"

"I will extol Thee, my God, O King: And I will bless Thy name forever and ever.
Every day I will bless Thee,
And I will praise Thy name forever and ever.
Great is the Lord, and highly to be praised;
And His greatness is unsearchable.
One generation shall praise Thy works to another,
And shall declare Thy mighty acts.
On the glorious splendor of Thy majesty,
And on Thy wonderful works, I will meditate.
And men shall speak of the power of Thine awesome acts:
And I will tell of Thy greatness.
They shall eagerly utter the memory of Thine abundant goodness;

And shall shout joyfully of Thy righteousness." Psalm 145: 1-7

INTRODUCTION

ﻬ ﻬ

This is not a devotional book although I hope it will lead you to worship Jesus in new ways as you meditate upon His power and purposes in your life. This is not a self-help book although I hope it will lead you to the One able to heal, forgive, restore and encourage you. This is not a school book although I hope it will lead you to a desire to be a student of God's book. Well then, what kind of book is it?? Good question! This is a book about miracles. Real miracles. By miracle I mean that the Creator of the universe purposely enters our ordinary days and does extraordinary things that only He can do!

Some of you will read this book and weep. Some of you will read what follows and grin or even chuckle. Some of you will read this book and initially shake your head in disbelief. Some may even read this book and think I have made all of this up!

May I say that no one could make this up. Actually, no one could even "think it up"!

My only request as you read the pages that follow is to keep an open mind and heart so the Lord of the universe can speak into your heart and spirit. Although there is no chronological order to the accounts that follow, most have occurred since 2004. And no matter when or where you are reading this, the final chapter has not yet been written.

Some of you may come to the last chapter and desire to know more about what the Lord is doing in West Africa. Some of you may want to know how to join Him in what He is doing there. Some of you may want information on opportunities of service through Shattering Darkness Ministries. The information found in this book will help you decide.

Shattering Darkness Ministries

> **« The Spirit of the Lord God is upon me, Because the Lord has anointed me to bring good news to the afflicted; He has sent me to bind up the brokenhearted, To proclaim liberty to captives, And freedom to prisoners.. To comfort all who mourn…Giving them a garland instead of ashes, The oil of gladness instead of mourning, The mantle of praise instead of a spirit of fainting. So they will be called oaks of righteousness, The planting of the Lord, that He may be glorified. »**
> **Isaiah 61:1-3**

Birthed in the heart of God. Founded upon the message of Christ as revealed in His perfect Word. Fueled by the flames of His Holy Spirit. Impacting unreached people groups in West Africa.

The Dagara and the Lobi and the Pougouli.. Who are they? Where are they? Who will reach The Dagara and the Lobi and the Pougouli, just three unreached people groups out of hundreds of unreached people in West Africa? Who will teach them? Who will play a part in their coming to Christ? Who will pay a part? Who will go to them? Who will send? Who will be the love of Christ for them? **Will you be the one???**

Located in Burkina Faso, Ghana and the Ivory Coast. They number more than 1.5 million people! They are primarily farmers, raising barely enough food each year to exist, never having an excess to sell. They are gentle, loving people enslaved by ancient practices and beliefs.

It is dark in their land. Oh, yes, the sun shines here. And yes, the moon and the stars shine here. There are oil lamps, flashlights, candles, matches and in some areas, there is even light from electricity. Yet their darkness is not dispelled by the sun or moon or stars or lamps. It is not physical darkness which ensnares them. It is something much worse and more dangerous. They live in spiritual darkness.

For centuries they have followed the practices of their ancestors: offering animal sacrifies, wearing sacred ornaments believed to protect them from evil spirits and illness, visiting witch doctors and fortune tellers. For centuries, they have lived and died in darkness. Nearly 1.5 million people... Jesus died for them...Jesus conquered the grave for them... Jesus bore their sins...Jesus loves them...Jesus wants to call them to Himself and save them. And yet even today, as you read this information...they are still in darkness...and most of them have never even heard His Name...

Who will shine His light, share His love, Tell of His life? **Will you be the one**?

It is cold in the land of West Africa. Oh yes, it is Sub-Sahara West Africa. Temperatures often between 90 to 110 degrees. But it is cold. So very cold. Oh, no, once again it is not physical coldness. It is much worse. These people live in spiritual coldness. For more than 100 years people have visited their land and their families. For more than 100 years foreigners have come and made promises. Promises to help them. Promises to feed them. Promises to build schools. Promises to bring health care. Promises to dig wells. Promises of a better life, a better way. These foreigners have promised to return. They lied. And with each visit, with each broken promise, with each passing year, West African hearts have grown more and more doubtful, more and more discouraged, more and more distrusting, more and more cold. So people are wary of the gospel. Does the gospel make 'promises' that will not be kept? Will the God of the Bible be any different than their gods?

Who will tell them the Truths of Christ? Who will live His truths among them? **Will you be the one?**

It is wet in the lands of West Africa. Oh, yes. It is dry here. It is dusty here. It is stony here. Year after year more and more of the Sahara desert encroaches and destroys. Yet the land is wet. Oh, no not physical wetness. No, their land is wet with the tears of parents watching their babies die of curable and even preventable diseases like malaria. It is wet with the tears of a few missionaries seeing the vastness of lostness and the absence of partners in prayer, partners in ministry, partners in giving. Most tragic of all, it is wet with the tears of heaven. The tears of our Beloved Savior looking upon a precious people for whom He came, He walked, He taught, He died, He rose again, He waits.....

And the Dagara and Pougouli and Lobi and Sisaala and Birifor and many others wait....to hear, to know, to call upon......His Name.

Who will speak His Name among them? Who will teach in His Name among them? Who will send in His Name? Who will sing in His Name? Who will love them in His Name? Who will touch them and comfort them in His Name? **Will you be the one**?

BUT WAIT......

I see a small flicker of light amidst the darkness. Ahh, I see a small group of people huddled around the last vestiges of dying embers. The people are afraid. They are cold. They hold to each other but do not speak. Their faces are bleak. Their eyes are dim, holding no hope, no joy, and no life.

WHAT IS THIS?

A small wind so faint it is barely noticeable. Yet it somehow makes it through the huddled group and fans the dying embers. The light becomes a bit stronger. There must be a little heat because the group moves away just a little. What is this? There is now room for someone else to join the small circle. And yes, the movement has allowed more of the small gentle breeze to reach the tiny flame.

The cycle continues.

More wind. More flames. More heat. More people. The people back away, making more and more room for others to join the group. More and more of the gentle wind reaches what is now a fire. The flames now alight upon the brush. The flames spread throughout the area. The wind (**or is it a breath?**) is much stronger now and the embers are being lifted into the air and alighting upon the trees and bushes which are now ablaze and burning bright and hot. So much more than a 'brush fire'. So much more than a forest fire. So much more.

As far as I can see...flames.
As far as I can see...people.

No longer fearful. No longer bleak. No longer without hope. No longer cold. No longer stationary. No longer alone.

IS THERE AN EXPLANATION??

Amidst the precious Dagara people group, our Holy God has released the breath of His Holy Spirit. The Holy Spirit has alighted and is calling the lost out of their spiritual darkness and into the Light of Jesus Christ. The flames continue to soar, seek and alight. The peoples need an opportunity to meet the Savior. They need to be given the opportunity to escape the cold, the wet and the dark. They should be given the opportunity to enter the warmth, the protection and the light of Christ.

Dagara believers are beginning to take the Light and Life of Christ into other people groups! They need training. They need materials. They need sponsors. They need prayer.

They need you.

Is God calling you to be a part of His miracle among these peoples? Does our Christ want you to be a 'torchbearer' amidst the darkness? Does our Christ want you to be the light of Christ amidst the darkness?

Does our Christ want you to be the one to prove the promises of the Scripture are true? To be the one teaching the Word of God? To be the one praying open the gates of heaven on their behalf? To be the one who will dry their tears?

To be the one who will heal their hurts? To be the one who will touch their skin? To be the one who will Shatter Darkness with the Life and Light of our Christ?

Will you be the one?

For information on how you can join the Ministries of Shattering Darkness, see our website located at: www.shatteringdarkness.org and follow the appropriate links.

Now, grab something to sip on, get comfortable, and enjoy the journey to a place close to the heart of God.

IN THE BEGINNING

❧ ❧

"The waters saw You, O God; The waters saw You, they were in anguish; the deeps also trembled. The clouds poured out water; the skies gave forth a sound; Your arrows flashed here and there. The sound of Your thunder was in the whirlwind; The lightnings lit up the world; The earth trembled and shook." Psalm 77:17-18

In the beginning....... God.

I do not know about other writers of God Stories. But I imagine any author struggles with the decisions of where to start and where to finish. There must be decisions as to what to include and what to delete. Most certainly when one desires to chronicle the Divine activities of God in personal lives, the decisions are most difficult. Yet start one must!

And so our journey begins. From the beginning. With God.

Shortly after I moved to the SW region of Burkina Faso ministry friends from America came to visit. Their visit coincided with another American couple as well. We were found one afternoon in the village of Navielgan. Navielgan was a very closed village with a lot of mockery and insults each time I visited them to share the love of Christ.

This particular afternoon was no different. Many people came to the meeting. Some actually listened to the lesson being taught. In Dagara culture, any person attending a meeting of any kind has the freedom to offer commentary or ask questions at the meeting's end. A man stood and spoke: "I want you to pray to your God and tell Him we need rain. We have planted our seeds. If it does not rain we will have no harvest!"

(No need to mention here my thoughts! "Why would you plant before the rains began? It is not even rainy season! What were you thinking?")

I responded by saying that we would pray. Yet I qualified my response and advised all who were there that our team would pray "Not for your crops, but so that you will know that what we have been teaching you about God is true. He is holy. He is powerful. He deserves our worship."

So we prayed. We prayed at the meeting. We prayed when we arrived home. I then sent an email to our American Partners in Prayer. Never before had I ever placed a time restraint on prayer! Yet I knew in this culture that if an extended period of time passed without rain, they would not recognize the hand of God when it did rain. I also knew that some would be going to a witch doctor and offering sacrifices to their "rain god" and would credit him for the rain! We really needed it to rain and to rain quickly!

I asked our Prayer Partners to ask God to send rain within 48 hours! I sent the email about 10 PM Burkina time which would have been 4-5 PM in the U.S. With bedrooms full with visitors, I went to sleep in my spare room on a couch facing the only window in the room. A short time later I collided with one of our visitors in the hallway. We had both been headed to close various windows in the house...because the rain was falling so heavily and powerfully the rain was coming into the house! Neither of us was able to speak! The thunder was so powerful the earth was shaking beneath our feet! The lightning was so frequent and far-reaching that the skies lighted up as if it was noonday!

When I finally got back to my room, I sat on the couch and looked out the small window into the heavens. I looked into the heavens our God created and kept repeating: "My God, I fear You. I fear You. I have no idea of Who You are, the depth of Your Holiness, the greatness of Your love! Oh! My God, I fear You!"

Early the next morning I piled my friends into the truck. I needed to see how far reaching the storms of the prior evening had been. As we approached the village of Navielgan it was easy to see the rains had reached them! It was also easy to see that a large group of people were gathered. When they spotted our truck they began running toward us. Before I was even able to get out of the truck the people were calling out "We believe! We believe! What you have told us is truth! We believe!"

I titled this chapter "In the beginning" for a specific reason. It was on this occasion that I began a new and much deeper reality walk with my Lord and Savior. He performs miracles! Miracles! Tangible, see-able miracles! He saw us. He heard us. He said yes. He transcended time and space and penetrated our world. His work of drawing an unreached people group named the Dagara to Himself was launched! He allowed us to witness the beginning of His call and activity within their hearts and lives. With this intervention He changed me as well!

THIS MIRACLE IS NOT ABOUT MONEY. It is about the God who loves. It is about the God who answers prayer. It is about the God who sees. It is about the God who forgives. It is about my God. I hope it is about yours as well!

GOD AWARENESS: Have you ever prayed and asked God for a miracle? Do you believe in the depths of your heart that He is capable of performing miracles? In the gospel of Luke chapter 1 verse 37 we read: **"For nothing will be**

impossible with God." Let us ponder this for a moment or two. Nothing. Nothing impossible. Nothing impossible with God. The key here is the phrase "with God." May it be that you and I will live from this moment forward trusting the One who walked on water. Trusting the One who calmed the seas. Trusting the One who knows us by name. Trusting the One who desires good things for us. Trusting Jesus.

In the space provided for you I want you to write out your request for God to do a specific miracle in your life or in the life of a loved one. I want this to be something for which God can provide a tangible, see-able answer. Perhaps you will ask for salvation for your spouse, family member or a co-worker. Perhaps you will request healing of a sick friend. Perhaps you will request finding a job. Perhaps you will request that your marriage be saved. Perhaps you will request that a wayward child returns home. Perhaps you will request being set free from bondage to drugs, alcohol or pornography. Be honest. Be specific. And in your request, ask God to give you the faith to believe that He still does miracles today!

_____

_____

_____

_____

_____

_____

_____

_____

_____

_____

_____

_____

_____

Let's Pray: Lord Jesus, Mighty Savior, Glorious King! We believe, Help our unbelief! Help us to trust You with the BIG things in our lives! Help us to believe You love and care and can be trusted. Please capture our hearts and lives and make them completely Yours. Please take us by the hand as we make this Faith Journey together! You and You alone are worthy of all praise and all honor and all glory! May the words of our mouths and meditations of our hearts be found acceptable in Thy sight, for Thou art our Hiding Place, our Strong Tower, our Confidant, our Hope, our Redeemer, our Song, Songwriter and the Music of our soul! In Jesus' Name, Amen and Amen!"

A CHANGE OF ADDRESS

❧ ❧

"For the ministry of this service is not only fully supplying the needs of the saints, but is also overflowing through many thanksgivings to God. Because of the proof given by this ministry they will glorify God for your obedience to your confession of the gospel of Christ, and for all the liberality of your contribution to them and to all." 2 Corinthians 9:12-13

The apostle Paul was a man of great faith. He was courageous. He was bold and brash. His life was transformed when Jesus called his name and saved his soul. Paul spent a LOT of time in prison. That may be the only reason we have so much of the New Testament! God had to corral him to get him to stay in one place long enough to write! You see, Paul absolutely loved His Savior. He was passionate to tell others about the true Miracle Worker. So Paul was quite often in a boat going from one continent to another in order to spread the gospel message.

I wonder if Paul got frustrated. Lonely? Angry? Confused? Or did he just get busy and make the most of the situation he was in??

I was a prisoner of sorts in 2005 and early 2006. Our ministry truck (19 years old at the time) had "died". Most of the ministry of Shattering Darkness involves "bush" villages which can not be reached by foot. So for all intents and purposes, I was housebound. The ministry continued and, in fact, expanded as our circuit-riding "bush" evangelists hopped on our dirtbikes and headed off toward the "ends of the earth". Once I got over pouting, I began writing. I love to write. I wrote and I wrote and I ended up with twenty new radio broadcasts and village lessons. I spent a good deal of time one-on-one with various leaders helping them to hone their skills in ministry. The year also found me doing a lot of counseling and writing lessons for our women's ministries.

Yet my heart was not happy nor fulfilled. One day I was reading in the book of Lamentations and read in Chapter 3 verse 17 *"My soul has been deprived of peace; I have forgotten what happiness is."* OH! That was it! That was my home address! And I had been living there far too long. I prayed and asked the Lord to show me what the problem was and how I could remedy it. I wanted to move back to my former address, joy and peace! The one that was in Christ's presence and at His side! The Lord led me to Revelation, chapter 2, verse 4. The Lord showed me that I had lost my passion for Him and His ministry. I was becoming lukewarm and sullen. As I sought to know how to remedy my staleness, the Lord showed me verse 5. *"Do the works you did at first".*

What had I done in the birthing stages of our ministry? I had taught the Bible in villages.

How I had loved discipling our new believers! Daily the truck was loaded with new believers for going to villages where they received genuine "on- the- front-line" training!

What did this all mean? I needed to get my eyes off my problems. I needed to ask forgiveness for my "self-fullness". I needed to fix my eyes on Jesus, the Author and Perfector of my faith! I needed to pray us a truck!

Pray us a truck?? In Burkina Faso in 2006 and 2007 a new Toyota pick-up was $40,000! No payment plan. Fifty percent with the placement of the order; pay in full on delivery of the truck! Our ministry is truly blessed with nearly 1000 people fervently praying on a regular basis for our ministry team. I contacted them and asked everyone to pray!

In 2006, I spent six months in the U.S. speaking in churches and ladies' meetings and Bible Study classes. I saved every penny in a separate account for the truck. Yet after 4 and a half months, there was barely $5,000. What to do?

The Global Impact Pastor of my home church was impressed by the Holy Spirit to propose a matching funds program, donating $20,000 toward the truck and contacting other pastors and churches to match the $20,000. The letter was to be mailed October 1, 2006 asking for a two week turn around to join in the effort.

THE MIRACLE: Sunday evening, September 30, Fellowship Hall (called *"FAITH HALL"* at our church); the last night of a week-long Missions Emphasis. A woman handed me $5,000 in cash saying the Lord had told her we needed the truck. At the same moment another woman was handing the Missions Pastor a check from her husband in the amount of $10,000 to place toward the truck. At the same moment another couple was approaching me saying "We have heard you still need $5,000; we have $5,000; we are giving $5,000!!!!!!

By this time I want you to know I was sobbing! The man's wife was sobbing! In the background I heard people whispering as they watched the miracle unfold, "It is ok. I think it is ok. She is ok. Those are happy tears!" With the other monies given, we were able to purchase a spare tire, insurance and front and rear guards!

Only a loving, gracious God would act in this way. To my way of thinking, it sure took a long time. Yet as I look back at it all…the Lord had a lot of work to do in my heart and life and it took time to get me where I needed to be. *YOU SEE, THE GREATEST MIRACLE OF ALL HAD NOTHING TO DO WITH MONEY.*

It had everything to do with God wanting to do something in my heart and life. He wanted to draw me back into a passionate relationship with Him. He wanted me to know Him as my Provider. He wanted me to ask for help. He wanted me to make needs known so others could be blessed by giving. He wanted me to leave my Faith 101 class and advance to Faith 202!! Only a loving, gracious God would act in this way.

GOD AWARENESS: I would like you to take a few moments and rehearse this miracle in your mind. What are you going through today as you read this chapter? What hurts are you experiencing? What doubts plague you? What needs do you have? God loves you. He wants to penetrate your heart and life. Will you let Him?

In the space provided, write one or two major things in your life that God and God alone can rectify.

_____

_____

_____

_____

_____

_____

_____

_____

_____

_____

_____

_____

_____

_____

_____.

Let's pray: "Lord Jesus. You are the Creator of all. You are the Giver of Life. You are the Sustainer of the weak and the Teacher of the seeking. You are the Light for those in darkness and You are the Hope of the hopeless. You own the cattle on a thousand hills. You know our needs today. We place them in Your hands and ask that while we wait for Your intervention, You show what we are to learn while in the 'waiting room'. In Jesus' Name we pray. Amen."

** Be sure to get a look at the photo of the Miracle Truck located in the Photo Gallery at the end of this book.**

NEW HOPE COMES
WITH A MOTO!

⊷⧼⧽⊶

**"Be anxious for nothing, but in everything by
prayer and supplication with thanksgiving let
your requests be made known to God." Philippians
4:6**

You have already read the story of our MIRACLE
truck... let me now continue by telling you about God's
New Hope Moto. A moto is also called a "bush bike" here. In
America we may say a "scooter." So in other words we are
not speaking of a large motorcycle or HOG! Our motos get
our evangelists to out-of-the-way places to share the Lord
Jesus and teach His Word.

Getting to remote villages is always a challenge. As
our ministry has expanded and more and more places have
"preaching points" (places where the Bible is taught weekly
but without an on-site pastor) the need to have motos available
is a real "ministry" in itself. Most of our church planter-
evangelists do their entire ministry with bicycles, but our
"circuit riders" need the motos to get where they need to
go.

It seems that having enough transportation is always an
item of prayer.

Two Shattering Darkness Board members came to spend a couple of weeks with us in March 2007. Their home church, New Hope Baptist in Fayetteville, Georgia, has been a partner with our ministry for several years. In addition to sending funds allowing us to purchase Bible Concordances for our key leaders and discipleship materials for our library at the Spiritual Formation Center (Phase I of III is now complete), they sent funds to purchase a new moto!

As these ladies come from "New Hope Baptist" and the moto is used exclusively for taking the message of Christ to the lost, it was natural to name it our New Hope Moto.

"So...this is a great story but where exactly is the 'miracle' in it??"

A few weeks after we received the moto and placed it in service for the Lord, some folks came and reclaimed a "moto-on-loan" to us for a different mission group to use. The Lord knew before we did how vital the New Hope moto would be! What would have happened if the New Hope moto had not been given?

In reality, ***THIS MIRACLE HAS NOTHING TO DO WITH MONEY!***

This miracle has everything to do with folks within the body of Christ responding to promptings of the Holy Spirit. It has everything to do with forming partnerships with mission agencies involved in indigenous ministry. It has everything to do with going to a lost world and arriving with the hope and message of the One who is able to break their spiritual shackles and lead them into the Light of Christ Jesus! Nothing to do with money. Everything to do with love and service and ministry.

GOD AWARENESS: I would like you to think about the last time you gave of yourself (time... prayer... clothing... Bibles...service...money) to help others in need. Can you think of someone even now who needs a touch from Jesus?

Are you willing to be the one God uses to meet their need?? (spiritually? emotionally? physically? monetarily?)

Write the name of the person or the family here. Now write specifically what you can do in the way of ministry. (Take a meal? Clean out the family closets and give clothing and shoes and toys to some needy folks? Visit someone in a nursing home? Volunteer to hold babies in the terminal illness ward? Perhaps join a local prison ministry outreach? Perhaps volunteer to be a monitor at a local school? Perhaps teach someone to read English?)

Write the "Who" and the "How" in the space provided.

_____

_____

_____

_____

_____

_____

_____

Let's Pray: "Lord Jesus. Thank You for meeting us where we have needs. Thank You for the sacrifice You endured and the price You paid in order to liberate us! Thank You for people You have placed in our lives during our times of need. Thank You for caring, for loving, for being the God of new beginnings and second chances. Now Lord, there are people all around me with unshed tears and unspoken needs. Lord, please help me to hear and to see them! Help me reach out to those who need You! Help me to be Your light in a dark place. Thank You, Lord Jesus. Amen"

** Be sure to see the Photo Gallery Section of this book to see the Moto as well as the Ministry Formation Center**

THE BLESSING of SPAM!!

⊰⧉⊱

"Now He who supplies seed to the sower and bread for food, will supply and multiply your seed for sowing and increase the harvest of your righteousness" 2 Corinthians 9:10

AND there is more! Our transportation needs were still not met…so we continued to pray. As we had been planning to reach a region of twenty-five non-evangelized villages, our church planting couple would begin with bicycles but we desired them to have a moto to facilitate them reaching the region of Zambo.

We continued to pray. One day I was getting gasoline and a "white" person approached me. It is a rare thing indeed to see white skin where I live. (I often forget I am white skinned!) It was a missionary I met years ago and he is a Bible translator. He told me he and his family were moving back to Switzerland permanently.

The same evening I received an email saying they had some things for sale in case I might be interested. One of the items he listed was a moto!!!!! I immediately responded by email that I would like the details. No response. I emailed again. No response. As this family lived in the "bush" and their departure date was quickly approaching I decided to take a ride to their home and took a mechanic along with me.

As we pulled up to their house, I saw the missionary in the front yard. I was pleased to find him at home. "Well, hello Lynn, I just responded to your email. It has been in my SPAM box. "Well now...why was it sitting in Spam, Lord? We could have settled all this by email or phone and I would not have spent all this time!"

The mechanic and I shared a meal with their family and we discussed many details of the moto, but did not talk about the price. I had the mechanic take it for a ride to be sure it was in good order. We then went back inside. The entire time I had an idea in my head of what we could afford to pay. I did not bring money with me because I did not want to have a lot of money in the truck with just me and a man I barely knew.

$1,500 would have been a super price. I thought we could probably pay $1,000. What were they asking for the moto?? The super price?? NO! The amount I thought we could scrape together? NO! You see, our Lord had set the price. Want to know how I know it was the Lord????? $462!!!!!! Yes, the missionary couple only asked $462.00!

Are you sensing the miracle here?

IT GETS EVEN BETTER

Before I left we had a time of prayer. The husband prayed and asked the Lord to use the moto to carry the "light of Christ" into dark places! Then his wife prayed and asked the Lord to provide for our widows and orphans. And then I prayed and asked the Lord to make their re-entry smooth and to provide friends quickly for their two young children. The wife was weeping as she held my hand. "I so needed you to come here today. Thank you."

As I headed home rejoicing in the purchase of a ministry moto, I realized why the emails had gone unnoticed and unanswered. Our loving Lord knew that this precious missionary mom would need someone that day. Did she need to hear someone to speak English with her? Maybe. Did this couple need someone they could vent with without fear of being judged or ridiculed? Did they need someone to discuss ministry stresses with? Maybe. Did they have doubts or fears and needed someone just to listen to their heart? Did they need someone to ask questions concerning leaving Burkina Faso and re-entry? Maybe. Or was it that they needed someone to pray for and with? Did they need to know that their time in Burkina Faso meant something? Did they need assurance that their time invested had not been in vain?

I do not have the answers. But I know that *THE BIGGEST MIRACLE OF THE DAY HAD NOTHING TO DO WITH MONEY*...it had everything to do with relationships, availability, spending time, listening, praying, caring and above all...being one in Christ our Savior.

GOD AWARENESS: I would like you to think about people currently in your life. This might be family or friends or co-workers or even someone in a Bible Study Group. Are you aware of problems or struggles or decisions currently in their lives? Write the names in the space provided.

_____

_____

_____

_____

_____

_____

I would like you to call or make a visit. Next, I would like you to listen to their hearts.

Then I want you to pray for them.

_____

_____

_____

_____

_____

_____

Now I want you to record who you spoke with, what you prayed and how they responded._____

_____

_____

_____

_____

_____

_____

_____

_____

_____

_____

Let's Pray: "Lord Jesus. You know our needs, wants and hurts. You know where we are bruised and bleeding. You know our doubts. You know decisions we are in the process of making. Thank You for allowing us to approach You without shame and without fear of rejection. Thank You that You are trustworthy and gracious. Please heal us Lord. Please show us who needs to be reminded of Your love and Your grace. Please keep them on our hearts until we reach out to them and pray for them. It is for the glory of Your Name that we ask these things Lord Jesus. Amen"

EATIN' IS BELIEVIN'

"Do not worry saying, 'What shall we eat?' or
'What shall we drink?' or 'What will we wear for
clothing?' For the Gentiles eagerly seek all these
things; for your heavenly Father knows that you
need all these things. But seek first His kingdom
and His righteousness and all these things will be
added to you." Matthew 6:31-33

My time of living and ministering among the Dagara
has been a real learning experience for me. Quite
often I find myself the learner and the new believers, the
teachers. Such was the case of the two young men from the
village of Movielo.

I had invited believers from about 15 villages to attend
a month long Bible course. I was doing daily biblical
teachings on topics like baptism, Lord's Supper, salvation,
marriage, purity and love. Each day covered one topic and
each evening there was homework.

The village of Movielo is off the beaten track and the
inhabitants were going hungry. Harvest was over and the new
planting season had not yet begun. The men of the village
scheduled a "hunt." All the men were to leave early in the
morning and hunt wild animals to kill, prepare and eat.

All of this was fine and very normal. However, the hunt was scheduled during the time of the Bible teachings. All the believers from village of Movielo, with the exception of two young men, opted to go look for food rather than attend the Bible lesson of the day. When the two returned home that evening it was dusk. They entered the village and found all the men had returned empty handed. They found the villagers upset that they had not joined in the search for food. Not even one rabbit had been found!

The two that had attended training decided to go out to the bush even though the others had found nothing. Even though it was almost dark, they wanted to try and find food. Remembering they had been taught to pray in faith believing God for their needs, they prayed. Before they had gone even a quarter of a mile the brush began to crackle and shake. The young men had their bows and arrows at the ready. And what came sauntering into clear view for easy pickin'?? A wild pig! A big, fat, wild pig!

The young men were so excited to return to their village with food to eat! Yet they did not keep their find only for themselves or their families. They called the villagers together, spoke of the faithfulness of God, and all shared in the feast!

THIS STORY IS NOT ABOUT MONEY. It is not about abundance. It is about the God who supplies our needs. It is about our God who rewards faithfulness.

It is about two new believers in Christ who hungered not for the meat of man but the meat of God's Word. And in the end they gained both!

GOD AWARENESS: How do we rank on the "Faith" scale?? Faithful in church attendance? Faithful in giving? Faithful in tithing? Faithful in praying? Faithful in serving? Faithful in studying the Word of God? When was the last time we placed God, His Word, His work, His people, His call *before* our own personal wants or desires? In the spaces provided I want you to write three places where you are spiritually in need of a "Faith Tune-up" and beside each place I want you to write what you can do in order to achieve victory. (Example: "I do not read my Bible every day" Corrective Action: "Read my Bible 5 minutes every morning before going to work")

1.) _____

Corrective Action _____

2.) _____

Corrective Action _____

3.) _____

Corrective Action _____

Let's Pray: "Father God, You know me. You know the world in which I live. You know how I am bombarded with false images and self-centered messages like "You deserve it. You are worthy. It is all about you. If it feels good, do it." And Father You know my proclivity toward greed and selfishness and excess. My constant desire for more, more, more. Oh! Father! Please create in me a new heart! A heart that yearns for You. A heart that desires You. A heart that is blind to the things of this world. A heart that breaks over the things which break Your heart. Please place within me a heart that is generous, a heart that is kind and a heart that will now beat in tune with Yours. I ask this Lord, because I so desperately need it, and so desperately desire You to be honored and glorified in me. This I pray in the Name of my Lord, Jesus. Amen."

BUILDING BLOCKS OF FAITH
MADE OF BRICK

€€

"But you, beloved, building yourselves up on your most holy faith praying in the Holy Spirit, keep yourselves in the love of God, waiting anxiously for the mercy of our Lord Jesus Christ to eternal life. And have mercy on some, who are doubting; save others, snatching them out of the fire; and on some have mercy with fear, hating even the garment polluted by the flesh. Now to Him who is able to keep you from stumbling, and to make you stand in the presence of His glory blameless with great joy, to the only God our Savior, through Jesus Christ our Lord, be glory, majesty, dominion and authority, before all time and now and forever. Amen." Jude 1:20-25

My years among the Dagara have taught me a lot about faith. They have taught me a lot about simple faith, childlike faith.

The men of the village of Kpakpara supplement their income by cutting bricks out of stone at a local stone quarry. It is hot, grueling, time-consuming work. Romaric was one of the men involved in the 30-day Bible training seminar.

He was also one of the men working at the quarry. Romaric decided to forego a month of work and income in order to learn more about the Word of God which he loved so much! When the training started, Romaric had approximately 100 bricks cut and carved and ready to be sold. In the second week of class he received word a man had come to his house and wanted to purchase some of the bricks. The man wanted 50 bricks and also required that Romaric hire a donkey and cart in order to deliver the bricks at the man's home. Romaric was thrilled! However, upon arriving at his home later in the day he discovered the man who wanted to purchase 50 bricks required Romaric to deliver them the following day. A seminar day. Romaric located the purchaser and explained his dilemma. He asked the man to wait for the week-end to take possession of the bricks. The purchaser refused! Romaric had no choice but to return the advance money the purchaser had left when he made the order.

The following morning Romaric was faithfully standing at the side of the road waiting for a ride to the training. He was joyful as always. His face shone with the joy and love of his Jesus! No one could have known by looking at his face that he had lost a substantial income for his family. Anyone seeing him would have seen a man content and fulfilled in life. They would have seen excitement and anticipation as he prepared to learn new things from the Bible he so treasured!

That evening he returned home to an amazing discovery. Another man had come to his house. This man wanted to purchase all 100 bricks! This man also brought his own truck and hauled away the bricks with no additional effort or work needed on Romaric's part!

THIS GOD STORY HAS NOTHING TO DO WITH MONEY. It has everything to do with a man who sought to know God above all other things. It is about a faithful God who knows and sees. It is a love story. A man and his God. God and His man.

GOD AWARENESS: We never know the lives and inner workings of people around us. We do not know their hurts or their needs. We do not know their sacrifices or their successes. We do not know their names. Unless we make the effort. Unless we listen, really listen when they speak. Unless we look in their eyes. Unless we ask. It is worth the effort! It is worth the investment! God is at work all around us. We will not see Him unless we risk becoming involved. Is there a homeless shelter in your town? A Crisis Pregnancy Center? A jail? A food pantry? A cancer ward at your local hospital? An AIDS clinic? An orphanage? A church nursery? In the space provided record some opportunities in your area where your touch, presence and prayers could impact a life.

_____

_____

_____

_____

_____

_____

_____

_____

_____

_____

_____

And what about world missions? Do you know a missionary? Do you know of a mission organization where your service and gift of time and resources could impact eternity? If you have answered yes, I encourage you to contact them and ask what you can do in order to meet a need.

Let's Pray: "Lord God, You are the Master Builder. And You build our faith one brick at a time. Make us Your apprentices, Lord Jesus. Help us to lay solid foundations of faith in our own lives and in the lives of others! Help us to build walls made of love and acceptance. Help us to place a roof of Sonlight and forgiveness. Help us to lay floors of softness and pliability. Help us to hang drapes of silk and beauty. Help us to paint doors and windows with the colors of Your rainbow! Help us to become a sanctuary. Your sanctuary! A place where You abide and where others are drawn to You! It is in Your Name, Lord Jesus, and for Your glory, that we pray. Amen"

I BELIEVE. HELP MY UNBELIEF!

⋘ ⋙

"And Jesus was going about in all Galilee, teaching in their synagogues, and proclaiming the gospel of the kingdom, and healing every kind of disease and every kind of sickness among the people." Matthew 4:23

Well now, I really do not like to "tell stories"… and this one is on myself no less!!!! People have such high regard for missionaries!! Here is something that happened about a year after I began ministry, so all involved (EXCEPT FOR ME) were new believers!!!!!!!

One day I made a drop-off stop in the village of Kpakpara. A team of new believers and I had spent the day in "bush" villages teaching the Bible. As I was dropping off the team, one of our believers came running across the road and it was evident he was coming with the news of some sort of emergency! He said we needed to pray. He said that someone in the village was dying. He said that we needed to plead with God for the sick man and to claim healing for him. His heart's desire was that God would heal him so that the hard hearts in Kpakpara would know God was real and powerful.

While still standing roadside, they grabbed hands (a new practice begun with my arrival) and began to pray. Oh! What a thrill; a band of men, all new in Christ, forming a circle of prayer in public! No shame. No hesitation. NO DOUBT. As they prayed beseeching God to show His power and glory and to heal this one close to death …..I was praying "Oh! God..they are so new in their faith! Please do not let them be discouraged when this person dies! Please do not let them lose faith! Please guard their hearts and spirits so they will be able to understand. "

So..imagine my shock, incredulity and shame when the next morning word came to me that the sick person was not only healed….but much, much more had occurred! While the prayer team was at his house praying for him, someone came and said, "Someone in my house is very sick. You must come and pray." Upon arrival at the second home, they discovered a young boy so sick he could not even sit up. As they began to pray, word again came about another gravely ill person. The young man immediately sat up, and in witness to the power of God, accompanied the prayer team to the third house!!!!! And yes!!!! God healed the third sick person!

I went before the Lord and prayed. I asked Him to forgive me. I said, "Lord…..I am the one who has walked with You for more than twenty years now. I know Your faithfulness and power and mercy and grace.

Yet it is this band of baby believers, new in faith that prayed..and believed..! OH! Here I am back in Faith 101 class! Father..I believe. Help my unbelief!"

We are now at the end of 2008. What has happened in the village of Kpakpara since this miracle of healing? Did it truly, as the new believer believed, open the village to receptivity for the gospel message??

We now have 5 acres on a plateau in Kpakpara. In January of 2008 we dedicated Phase I of our Ministry Formation Center, which included a well, a house of worship and a Bible

Study building for the youth! Since then we have also added an outdoor baptismal pool in the form of a Cross! Included in our long-range plans are two dormitories, a Christian school, a Training center with library and a pastor's house as well as housing for our future school teachers.

THIS MIRACLE HAD NOTHING TO DO WITH MONEY. Nor did it have anything to do with spiritual maturity, seminary training or development.

It had everything to do with a God who loves enough to transcend time and space, logic and experience...in order to open eyes, touch hearts and save the lost!!

GOD AWARENESS: Are you facing situations today that seem "impossible" to you? Maybe you have been praying for a very long time for someone to accept Christ as Savior. Maybe you or someone you love suffers from a chronic illness. Perhaps you need a job and are weary with countless rejections. Is it that you have a wayward child? Is it that your marriage is crumbling apart? God knows! He sees! He cares!

I want you to spend some time thinking about the sorrows and challenges in your life. Choose one of them to pray about. Are you willing to fast and pray? Are you willing to believe? God is waiting to do miracles in your life!

Let's Pray: "Lord Jesus. You walked on water! You healed the sick! You delivered people from demons! You fed the hungry! You raised the dead! You rose again from death and the grave! You were and continue to be the Conqueror! We BELIEVE!!!!! Please help our unbelief. Lord Jesus, we pray and believe in Your Name. Amen"

SHE HAS A NEW NAME

❧ ❧

"He executes justice for the orphan and the widow,
and shows His love to the alien by giving him food
and clothing." Deuteronomy 10:18

Here where I live in Burkina, children are often named
as a result of the birth experience or perhaps something
that happens shortly after birth. Thus, our encounter with a
very sick baby whose momma had died shortly after giving
birth. The baby was given the name "Insulted". Imagine!
A child will be insulted every time her name is called. All
her life she will be reminded she is blamed for her mom's
death!

She was brought by her grandmother at the end of a
"bush" village meeting to some visitors from America. The
grandmother asked them to pray for the baby. Although only
a few months old, the tiny one looked to be just days old!

Well, now, this will never do! I went to grandma and told
her it was impossible for us to accept the name. We asked
permission to change her name. They gave us permission.

In the days, weeks and months that followed we took
the baby to a malnutrition center about 50 kilometers from
the home village. Later, when the grandmother refused to
bathe and feed her, she was transferred to a center closer to

53

my home and we found a widow from one of our churches willing to be a surrogate momma!

(We discovered later that grandma had been beating and starving her! When she knew we were coming for the baby, she ran away trying to hide from us and to keep us from saving the life of the baby. Her ancient thoughts told her that her daughter would come back to look for the baby!)

God so graciously intervened and allowed her birth father and one of our pastors to find them much later the same day. The pastor brought the baby to us. She had gone all day with not even a drop of water on her lips!!!!

I took her into my arms and wept! I pleaded with the little one to keep fighting. I kept telling her how sorry I was! I kept saying: "Do not stop fighting. Do not stop. Do not stop. We are here now."

In the initial weeks, she would cry every time there was no bottle at her mouth! I guess she thought she would never be fed again!

I am writing this as she turns 18 months of age! She and her "momma" spent 8 months at the malnutrition center and were just recently released to go "home". The baby is fat, laughing and playing with toys. She likes riding in the truck going to church. She has recently started putting her hands together when we sing praises! She giggles. She has about 8 teeth.

Due to the gracious giving from a ladies Bible Study group in the U.S., we recently finished building a house for her "momma" Madeline and Madeline's two teen-aged children.

Well, now.....for how many paragraphs have you been asking yourself "what is her name?" "What is her name?" Think I forgot to tell you??

Be patient just a little longer and I will tell you. We wanted her to have a name that would speak blessing to her every time someone spoke her name. We wanted her to have a name that would also be a testimony and give her value.

Her name in Dagara is Naamwin Chilo. In English her name means: "God's Joy and Delight." And indeed we are convinced she is exactly that to the One Who miraculously allowed us to be in the right place at the right time. *THIS MIRACLE HAS NOTHING TO DO WITH MONEY.* It has everything to do with a God Who knows and sees and transcends time and space to change eternity!

GOD AWARENESS: Do you know any orphans or widows?? I imagine you do. Most of us do. Or perhaps you know of someone that has adopted a child? Take a few moments and ask the Lord what you can do specifically for one of them that would be a blessing for them, a privilege for you, and an honor to our God.

Write it here. Then write the date once you have completed the task!

_____

_____

_____

_____

_____

_____

_____

_____

Let's Pray: "Lord God. We were all spiritual orphans until the moment You adopted us into Your family!! Thank You that we now wear Your Name. Help us Lord to represent You in a way that will bring glory to Your Name and pleasure to Your heart. Help us Lord to be conscious of hurting people found all around us. Help us Lord to minister to their needs and be faithful in praying for You to heal their hearts and spirits. In Jesus' Name we pray. Amen"

** You can see a photo of God's Joy in the Photo Gallery of this book**

AESHA

❧ ❧

"This is pure and undefiled religion in the sight of our God and Father, to visit orphans and widows in their distress, and to keep oneself unstained by the world." James 1:27

People often ask me to describe what an "ordinary day" is like for me. I never know how to answer that! After all, I live in a bush village in the small country of Burkina Faso, West Africa. Until quite recently, there was little or no electricity. My water comes from a well. To have a hot shower entails heating water on the stove. My kitchen has no sink and no running water. My refrigerator is in my living room. I may not know how to explain an ordinary day, but let me try and explain one of my "supernatural days".

It was a typical day in that I was in the truck. Some Dagara leaders were with me and we were headed back to our small town after teaching the Bible in a far away place. As we were traveling, one of the young men asked if we could stop and pray for a woman who was very ill.

When we arrived at the village of Bonchiol we found the sick woman, Kpiero, and her daughter Aesha. Kpiero, whose name meant "Suffering", was dying of AIDS. Her husband had already died and the family was refusing to admit she was even a family member! We prayed with her and asked the village chief for permission to come again and to share God's word with them the next visit.

This began a twice-weekly visit during the months that followed. One of our female leaders accompanied me and helped me as we bathed Kpiero, washed her mat and her clothing, applied ointment to her emaciated body and fed her with food we brought with us. All the while people watched. All the while no one offered to help. During these months, we shared the gospel with Kpiero and anyone else who would listen. Her daughter, Aesha, was always there and always at her momma's side.

On one visit Kpiero told us she would accept Christ if He would heal her! Later she said she wanted Jesus to forgive her whether or not He healed her! The day Kpiero prayed to receive Christ, we told her she had a new name! We told her that her name was now "Kpiero Bara" which means "your suffering is over". Kpiero died a few weeks later. I spent the night of the funeral at the village and precious Aesha never left my side.

In the months that followed, it was very difficult to keep track of Aesha. Family members kept shuffling her from one place to another. During the two years that we ministered to Aesha and continued weekly in the village of Bonchiol, some Impact Teams from First Baptist Church, Dillon S.C. came to know and love Aesha. In a recent meeting the team led Aesha to know Jesus as her Savior!

The heart of one of the team members, Craig, was deeply touched with the needs and the suffering of Aesha. Aesha was being passed around by various family members. She was being treated like a servant rather than a relative. It was often difficult for us to even know where she could be found. We began to seek the heart and mind of God concerning Aesha, her future, and our role in her life. Upon returning to the U.S., Craig spoke with his wife and they made a commitment to provide clothing and schooling for Aesha. In mid

July 2008 we received permission from an uncle for Aesha to move and live with one of our pastors, his wife and baby!!!

Aesha is now living in the village of Nakar, attending school, wearing new clothes and has recently joined the youth choir at church! I await the day when Aesha will giggle and laugh. I await the day that she realizes the Lord will never abandon nor forsake her! I await the day when she will give and receive hugs.

In a recent study of the word **"visit"** in the Scripture verse noted above I discovered that the meaning of the word in the Greek language means far more than to go and visit someone at their home or office. The word can literally mean: care for, care about, to relieve, to inspect, to select or to see. In other words, it means to become involved in a person's life and in their suffering! It means to make a purposeful emotional investment as well as time and perhaps money.

Was the day we stopped to pray for Kpiero a normal day? I am not sure. Was it a supernatural day with eternal impact? Without a doubt. *IS THIS MIRACLE ABOUT MONEY? NO!* Is this miracle about the love of God? Yes! Yes! Yes!

GOD AWARENESS: I believe there are people all around us with hurts and needs. Do we see them? Do we even look? We make time for things important to us. Let us make an effort to truly look in peoples' eyes and listen to their hearts! Hug someone today. Take someone to lunch this week. Invite someone to church this coming Sunday. Has the Lord placed someone on your heart? Write their name and their need in the space provided.

_____
_____
_____
_____
_____
_____

_____

_____

_____

_____

_____

Let's Pray

"Lord Jesus. Thank You for allowing Aesha's mom to come to know You. Thank You that we know her suffering is over and she is with You. Thank You for allowing Aesha to be in a Christian home. Thank You that she is growing in faith and hope as she learns more and more about Who You are! How we look toward and long for the day when Aesha will laugh! How we long to see her run and play. Lord God, how easily we forget the widows and orphans that You love so deeply! Help us to see them Lord. Help us to love them. It is in Your glorious Name we pray. Amen."

Please write additional thoughts you may have had while reading Kpiero Bara's and Aesha's story.

_____

_____

_____

_____

_____

_____

_____

_____

_____

_____

_____

_____

_____
_____
_____

** Be sure to see a photo of Aesha located in the Photo Gallery section at the end of this book**

ADOPTED!

སྐ་ ལྐ་

"But when the fullness of the time came, God sent
forth His Son, born of a woman, born under the
Law, so that He might redeem those who were
under the Law, that we might receive the <u>adop-
tion</u> as sons, God has sent forth the Spirit of His
Son into our hearts, crying, "Abba! Father!"
Therefore you are no longer a slave, but a son;
and if a son, then an heir through God." Galatians
4:4-7

Throughout my years of ministry in Burkina Faso, the
Lord has blessed me with opportunities to meet and to
partner with incredible people and incredible churches! At
times, our relationships begin long before we meet face to
face. This God Story is about one of them.

In early 2008 I received an email from one of our
Board members. She informed me that a man in her church
was inquiring about the purchase price of a motorbike for
Shattering Darkness Ministries. Later the same week the man
went to her office again and said the Lord had not released
him, stating the Lord also desired for he and his wife to pay
for the digging of a well in the village of Naro. This senior
adult couple began praying for the village and the pastor and
leaders by name.

Late in 2008 I had the opportunity to meet this couple face to face when I visited their church. What a thrilling time that was! As we spoke privately I asked them to pray with me and for me for a sad situation which had developed in Naro. A ministry had promised to build a house of prayer for us in Naro and in two other villages. However, when it came time for the construction to begin, only two churches could be built!

Our believers in Naro were heartbroken! For more than 8 years they had been meeting! They began as all new-work villages begin..meeting under a tree. From there they constructed a small shade roof. A few years later they shaved dry corn stalks and hauled dry tree limbs and constructed a thatched church. When they received news of a church building they were elated. When they received news that the church would not be built they were devastated. We spoke with them and encouraged them to keep praying and keep believing.

As I spoke with the couple who had already paid for the scooter and the well, the husband began to weep. Then he said "I have to do this. I have to do this." Looking to his wife he said: "We have to do this. We have to do this." She smiled knowingly and responded, "I know."

The following morning as we were gathering for Bible Study, this Faith Partner greeted me and said he had already given an envelope to our ministry Treasurer to pay the full construction price of the church in Naro! In addition, he said he had written me a note and to be sure I got it. With his permission, I copy his note in the paragraphs to follow. It is not so much *his story* as it is a *God Story!*

"Dear Lynn,

All my youth was spent in an orphanage. I never really had anything I could call my own. At the age of nine I came to know Christ. My nights were spent on my knees. When I prayed I asked God that if it was possible to <u>please</u> provide for me an education, a Christian wife (that could love an orphan), a house, a son and a daughter, and finally a good job so that I could take care of the family He gave me. Need I say that every prayer was heard and the blessings ten-fold? I have found it an easy thing to give away what I have for in those years I had only what God provided.

I learned that God loved me and He could love me through others. "Jesus loves me!" was the thought that carried me during those years. I knew I had *nothing* but *Christ* to face an uncertain world. When a commitment is made and for some reason it falls through, God has someone "standing in the wings" to provide help.

When you tell of your experiences and the needs for His Kingdoms' work, my heart is touched..just as it was when I heard a missionary speak when I was a child. I could do nothing to help then because I had nothing. Because of His blessings, I can respond now as I wanted to respond back then. "Oh, thank You Lord, for allowing me to be the one "standing in the wings."

As I said, when you speak of the needs in Burkina Faso the Holy Spirit rips at my heart. I am brought to tears when in the Presence of the Holy Spirit. How awesome to be surrounded by His Spirit! "Thank You, Lord! I will "stand in the gap!" I will make a commitment and follow through. Oh, God. How can I do less?"

As I lay awake last night my thoughts were about Naro. In my mind's eye I could see Alexis and Georgette and their baby. I could see Simplice, Jean Clemente and their families. There are so many needs the world over and we want to make a difference in a small spot. I thought if we could just "beam" over *and* meet at their "new" church *and* give each one a sack lunch *and* sit *and* eat with them *and* sing a song *and* have the Lord's Supper *and* pray together....how wonderful that would be! Then, we would look each one in the eyes and say "We Love You!" Could it be possible, would it mean as much to them as the reality that I was loved by Jesus meant to me as a child?

Please do this for me, for us. Celebrate Jesus at the new church being constructed to the glory of God in Naro! Have a meal. Pray. Sing. Dance. Please tell them that Jesus loves them. Please tell them that we love them. Thank you for going! We continue to pray for you."

THIS GOD STORY IS NOT ABOUT MONEY. It is about the grace and faithfulness of our Lord! He saw an orphan. He knew his name. He called him into relationship and family! No longer an orphan! No longer fatherless! Abba, Daddy!

GOD AWARENESS: Have you ever found yourself feeling alone and forsaken? Have you ever felt that no one, God included, cared about you? No one knew what you were feeling? No one understood? Perhaps even as you read this you are thinking, "That is how things are for me right this moment!" Take heart. God knows. God sees. God cares. Even if it does not *"feel"* that way, He does! He loves you. He is always ready for us to draw near to Him. He is always ready to forgive us. He is always ready to accept us. He is always ready to give us a fresh, new start. He is always ready to comfort us.

Please take a few moments to be still. Please allow the Lord time to speak to your heart. Please allow God time to touch and heal the places in your heart and spirit where you are bruised and bleeding. Hmm….still doubting that God truly loves you? How about this: 2 Samuel chapter 22 verse 20*: "He also brought me forth into a broad place; He rescued me because He delighted in me."* Wow! Our Creator God..delights in us!! Still doubtful? Ok. How about this: *"The Lord your God is in your midst. A victorious warrior, He will exult over you with joy, He will be quiet* *in His love, He will rejoice over you with shouts of joy"* (Zephaniah 3:17) Wow! Wow! Still not sure?

"For God so loved _____(put your name here), **that He gave His only begotten Son,** *that* _____ _____ (your name here) *believe in Christ will never perish, but that* _____ ___(your name here) *would have eternal life."* Jesus Christ, the risen Son of God delights in you! He exults over you with joy! He died in your place, a payment for your sins! He is alive! Believe it! Accept it! Receive it!

Record what you are feeling in these moments:

_____
_____
_____
_____
_____
_____
_____
_____

Let's Pray: Lord Jesus, in moments like these I find it difficult to express what I so desperately want You to know! To say "Thank You" seems almost crude because it falls so far short. To say "I love You" seems meaningless when compared to Your love for me! So it seems better just to ask You to see my heart, soul and spirit. Please know those things I can not adequately say! May my life and desires and service be a reflection of Who and What You are to me! Help me to love and adore and exalt You in the manner You and You alone are worthy! And this I pray in Your magnificent Name, Jesus! Amen."

FALLING INTO GRACE

⋐✿ ✿⋑

"Bless the Lord, O my soul; And all that is within me, bless His Holy name. Bless the Lord, O my soul, And forget none of His benefits; Who pardons all your iniquities; Who heals all your diseases; Who redeems your life from the pit; Who crowns you with lovingkindness and compassion." Psalm 103:1-4

My home church in America is BIG! In the years I have been away since I left for Bible training and the mission field in 1990, the pastor under whose ministry I came to a personal relationship with Jesus had retired. I thus arrived in 2006 to a new pastor. He did not know me. I did not know him.

Yet before I met him I loved him. How could that be?? Because I read something he wrote and I knew without ever having spoken with him that we were kindred spirits. In a church newsletter pastor's column he wrote: "The mark of a great church is not how many people it seats. The mark of a great church is how many people it sends!!"

A pastor of a 10,000 member mega church does not find himself wanting for things to do. Yet in November 2007 he wrote me an email. In the email he said that he was asking God to protect and heal me and referenced Psalm 103. He could not know that the following day I would fall, tear some ligaments in my foot (4 days before the arrival of our first-time ever area-wide Evangelistic Crusade Team!!) and be laid up until the moment I headed to the city for the team.

The day of the accident, sent from Ghana the exact moment I was injured, the director of Ministry and Missions for Shattering Darkness was sending me an email thanking me for the investment I was making in his people group and saying he was praying that God would protect me and encourage my heart! He referenced Psalm 103!

There is still more!!

As I was pretty much captive to a chair at my desk for three days, I had a lot of time to clean out some boxes and put some things in order. The day following the accident I noticed a small slip of tattered paper on the floor. It was blank and about the size of a business card. As I picked it up to toss it away, I noticed the writing on the reverse side. "Praise the Lord Lynn (No kidding' it has my name!! Look at the photo in the Photo Gallery) and then because the card was tattered, I saw bits and pieces from Psalm ......mmmhmm 103:1-4!!!!! I was stunned! Speechless. Then I realized that although totally alone I was grinning ear to ear and began to...well, ok...

I actually began to giggle!!!!!!! I have the card taped to my computer so that I NEVER forget the **Master'**s personal **Miracle** in a time of physical need!!!!

You see, *THIS MIRACLE HAD NOTHING TO DO WITH MONEY.* It had everything to do with God knowing I was injured. It had everything to do with God knowing I was discouraged and close to panic. It had everything to do with God meeting me at the place of my need.

It also had to do with God touching the heart of my pastor and the heart of our ministry Director and prompting them to contact me. His Holy Spirit prompted them both to be praying for my health! The day prior and the very moment of the accident! Only God could know!

GOD AWARENESS: I want you to think of a time that God intervened in your life. Maybe something that you had forgotten until reading this chapter. Maybe something you never realized was God until just now! I want you to write a few words below that will prompt you to remember now and again that God loves you so much He uses people to hug you and touch you and speak to you in ways only God could have known you needed!

_____

_____

_____

_____

_____

_____

_____

_____

Let's Pray: "Dear Lord Jesus, we are once again before You. We want to thank You for being active and personal in our lives. Thank You for the way You protect us, many times without our knowledge. Thank You for the way You use people to be Your emissaries in our lives! Thank You for Your Holy Spirit and the way He moves our hearts and spirits. Thank You. In Your glorious Name we pray. Amen."

Is there more you wish to say to our Lord? Write it to Him in the space provided.

_____

_____

_____

_____

_____

_____

_____

** Be sure to see the Scripture card located in the Photo Gallery in this book**

THE BURIAL POOL

⚓⚓

"Do you not know that that all of us who have been
baptized into Christ Jesus have been baptized into
His death? Therefore we have been buried with
Him through baptism into death, in order that as
Christ was raised from the dead through the glory
of the Father, so we too might walk in newness of
life. For if we have become united with Him in the
likeness of His death, certainly we shall be also in
the likeness of His resurrection." Romans 6:3-5

This *GOD* story actually began shortly after Jesus rose
from the dead!

It continued at a time shortly after the end of World War
II!!

It continued in the summer of 2006 when I purchased a
Study Bible containing lots of photos of antiquities in the
Bible lands.

It continued in the summer of 2007 as one day I was
reading in Romans chapter 6 and looked at a photo of an
ancient "death pool" or "burial pool"! All the air left my lungs
as though I had been smacked by a two by four. I looked!
And I knew the Lord wanted us to dig a "burial pool" for our
baptisms! I contacted the builder of our ministry church and
office and said I needed to see him. I showed him the photo

of the burial pool that must be about 1,500 or more years old and said I wanted him to draw up plans for one.

This *GOD* story continued along the road from the capital city of Ouagadougou to our area of Diebougou in the southwest of Burkina Faso that same fall. I had Rev. Larry McFadden and his Crusade team in the Miracle Truck. Larry and I have known each other for years and it was wonderful to do a little catching up. Before I knew it, without prior knowledge of my hopes and plans, he was telling the following story concerning 'burial pools":

A British colonel who had been given the assignment after WW II of retracing the steps of the Nazi generals from Hitler began to find these holes dug in the ground in the shape of a cross. He found these in many of the villages that had been destroyed by the Muslims. After seeing several of these cross-shaped holes in the ground, the British colonel finally found a man who said, "These are called burial pools". Then later another man said, "The burial pools come from the teaching of the Ethiopian." So it seems likely the Ethiopian, found in Acts 8, discipled and sent out missionaries, and they baptized people with their hands outstretched as if they were being crucified on a cross. What a picture! And the Ethiopian impacted a continent for Jesus because Philip was obedient to "go down that desert road." (Enjoy reading Acts 8:25-40)

I was so excited!! I let my friend know that I had something to show him as soon as we arrived at the house! First I showed Larry, Bob and his wife, Linda, and Paul the photo in the Bible! Then I showed them the builder's plans already completed!

An Ethiopian met Jesus as Savior on a desert road. It is apparent he did not keep silent. Little did he know that his influence and faithfulness would touch a continent! I doubt he ever imagined a photograph. And now in April of 2008, we have had our first baptisms in our "burial pool".

THIS MIRACLE IS NOT ABOUT MONEY. It is about the difference *one life* can make. It is about the significance *one life* can have.

Is *your life* impacting eternity? Is mine?

GOD AWARENESS: Many years ago there was a popular song which inquired "will those who come behind us find us faithful"? Beloved, let that be our hearts' cry today. That those being touched by our lives find that we have faithfully followed our Savior. May we leave a legacy of faith and faithfulness. A legacy of boldness and perseverance. A legacy of love and courage. A legacy resounding with the message, hope, light and glory of our Savior!

In the space provided for you please record the ministry or the service or the activity you are currently involved in which legacy is building. Then record in what ways this effort is impacting eternity. If you do not see yourself currently involved in Kingdom matters please pray and ask the Lord to lead you to a place of service.

_____

_____

_____

_____

_____

_____

Let's Pray: "Lord Jesus. I want my life to have an eternal impact on a lost world. Is this a selfish prayer, my King? My heart burns with the desire that all should hear Your Holy Word! My spirit burns with the need to be the one who says like Isaiah "Here am I, Lord, send me!" Oh, my Beloved Savior...lostness is all around me! On these desert roads! In these schools! In these courtyards! On my front porch! Needing to know You. Needing to turn from old ways. Needing to leave ancient practices. Fearing You more than they fear their false gods! Loving You more than they love themselves and fleshly desires. Oh, My Savior, please, please use me up in Your fields white unto harvest! Pour me out upon a dry and thirsty land. Oh, lovely Jesus, burn me up with an intensity that is greater than the very fires of hell in my quest to take You and Your Word and Your light into the midst of darkness! Please, Father. Please. Until the day when every knee shall bow and every tongue confess to the glory of God the Father that Jesus Christ is Lord! Amen!"

Read Romans chapter 6.

** Be sure to see the photo of the Burial Pool in the Photo Gallery Section**

A LONG WAY FROM HOME

∽❧ ❧∽

"Unless the Lord builds the house, They labor in
vain who build it; Unless the Lord guards the city,
the watchman keeps awake in vain." Psalm 127:1

Our ministry had blossomed and expanded incredibly
since 2004. Sadly, many of our areas were still meeting
under trees or a lean-to. Building churches just was not an
option financially for our ministry.

One day some friends, fellow missionaries, stopped by
for a short visit. Tami said to me, "You should try to get in
touch with Madame Kim. She lives in the city of Bobo and
she builds churches. We recently attended the dedication of
one of her church buildings."

Sound easy?? Things to bring glory to God are not
usually easy and this was no exception. I was able to get the
phone number of a pastor in her area. He then was able to
give me her number. I called and called and called. One day
months later, someone answered the phone. I was informed
that Madame Kim was in Korea and would be gone a few
months.

A year later. Nothing. Then one day the same friends
stopped in and in the course of conversation they asked if I
had ever touched base with her. "She must still be out of the

country" was my reply, "because I left numerous messages for her to call upon her return".

My friends responded by saying, "Between our place and yours we passed three new churches she has just completed. She must be in-country."

By this time, we had three couples attending Bible School in the city where Madame Kim lives. We also discovered she and the Director of the school often worked together. Working with the Director and our students, we were finally able to contact her. The Director of Ministry and Missions and I made an appointment to meet with her on January 15, 2008.

A bit of her story, as she herself expressed it:

"While I lived in Korea, we participated in a church building project. Our members joined together and we built a five story building which cost more than $1 million dollars. Shortly afterwards, many of the faithful fell away. Much discord developed.

A while later my husband moved the family to Burkina for his work. I did not come here as a missionary or with a mission in mind. A short time later we visited a church...my heart broke! How could this be called a church? A place to worship my Savior? This is a place for the animals, NOT a place for my Savior!

I turned my back and closed my eyes. Yet daily in my prayer times the church 'building' kept coming back to me. I kept my eyes closed and my back turned. The Holy Spirit kept telling me to do something to help. My husband was in agreement so we helped the struggling band of believers to build a church.

All of a sudden, pastors from all over Burkina Faso were showing up at our door!

They brought with them photos of their "churches". Trees... or limbs with grass roofs....or mud bricks... ' oh,

NO!' my spirit cried. 'These are places for the animals...not for Jesus!'

I prayed for forty days and I fasted forty mornings! I wept! I cried out to my God! I am poor, I told Him. What can I possibly do?

On the forty-first day my phone rang. It was someone from Korea. He told me his name. He asked if I was the woman who builds churches. Then his group sent us money! A few days later the phone rang. It was a man in Germany. He said I did not know him but he had heard I build churches. His group sent money. A few days later, a call from America! 'Are you the woman who builds churches in Burkina Faso?" They sent money. And now today we have completed 150 church buildings!!!!!! Oh, not me! I am only a poor woman. It is Jesus. All Jesus!"

Madame Kim arrived here in Sept of 1996. So did I! Korea is a long way from Burkina Faso. America is a long way from Burkina Faso. Yet here we were, nearly eleven years later and meet face to face for the first time! I sensed immediately I was in the presence of a godly, impassioned woman. She has known much heartache in these years but has remained tenacious in faith and faithfulness. Her eyes filled with tears as she said, "Please pray. Pray for your churches. Pray for the villages. Have your believers praying even now.

Pray against the onslaught of satan sure to follow. Please pray for me.

The battle is so ferocious. I get headaches. My son, a pastor, just died in a plane crash......please pray for me."

I promised her we have been and will continue. I then said perhaps one day her testimony will have an update "and now as of today we have built 150 Dagara churches!"

I am truly humbled this night. What a privilege to be with her.

One lady, (in every sense of the word), Her Savior. Impacting Burkina for eternity!

My tears fell freely as she spoke. I prayed...I pondered.... I was breathless...I was changed and am challenged today. It is May 21, 2008 as I write this. Madame Kim should be in Burkina by the end of the month. The construction of two Dagara churches will begin immediately upon her return!

** The church in the village of V-1 was dedicated to the glory of God in late July, 2008! The house of worship in the village of Tenkiedougou was dedicated in early July, 2008!

THIS MIRACLE IS NOT ABOUT MONEY. It is about listening to God. It is about one woman. A poor woman. And her love for her Savior.

GOD AWARENESS: Take a few moments to reflect... honestly. When you attend worship at your local church, do you go in order to "be blessed" ....or to "be a blessing?" Do you pick apart the message or allow the Holy Spirit to speak to you through the Scriptures? Do you appreciate having a place to worship? Do you thank God for the folks who vacuum and clean and polish? Do you attend with an attitude of worship or to socialize? I want you to take a moment to thank the Lord for all who serve Him in making your church building a place where you can have fresh encounters with the Living God!

In the space provided, record the name of your Pastor and your Bible Study leader. Name any others within your church who have a part in your discipleship. Once you have recorded their names stop and pray for them. Thank God for them. The next time you see them let them know you had special prayer on their behalf! _____

_____

_____

_____

_____

_____

_____

_____

_____

_____

_____

_____

Let's Pray: "Lord God, we come before You in these moments ashamed at our inconsistencies and passionless forms of worship! Father, please forgive us for our selfishness, judgmental hearts and complacent spirits! Please cleanse us with the Saviors' blood shed at Calvary. Please forgive our arrogance and pride! Please take us by the hand and lead us back to the foot of Calvary's Cross and meet us there. Teach us there. Renew us there. Assign us our tasks there. Empower us there. Fill us to overflowing with the power and presence of Your Holy Spirit there. Replace our callousness with fiery passion for You there! We ask this, we plead for this in the Name above all names, Jesus. Amen."

** Be sure to see the picture of Madame Kim in the Photo Gallery**

THE LIVING WATER

༄ ༄

"Jesus answered and said to her, 'If you knew the gift of God, and who it is who says to you, 'Give me a drink' you would have asked Him, and He would have given you living water...whoever drinks of the water that I give him shall never thirst; but the water that I shall give him shall become in him a well of water springing up to eternal life.'" John 4:10, 14

Water of any kind is scarce here in Burkina Faso. Our rivers dried up many years ago. We have no lakes. One gets excited when it rains and we see a puddle! The kids run out of doors and splash and giggle and dance in the rain! OK, so it is not only the children! We all rejoice and dance in the rain when we have the first rain of the season, which often comes after six to eight long months with no rain at all!

We do not have many wells here in Burkina. And many of the ones we do have are old and crumbling. Others have never been capped and thus are now contaminated. Some people walk 1-2 miles to find a well that has not dried up or fallen in or been contaminated.

In the summer of 2007 a former missionary to Burkina Faso called me from the United States. He wanted to know if we were interested in or had need of some wells being drilled. Oh! Yeah! The next few months found me doing a lot of research and gathering a lot of information and statistics.

Once the project proposal was submitted...nothing happened. Nothing that was visible that is. In the meantime, we hand dug a well at our ministry site in the village of Kpakpara.

A few months later two of our Shattering Darkness Board members contacted me saying a man from their church had donated money for us to dig a well! Today is May 21, 2008 and we just finished capping another hand dug well in the village of Naro. They had to dig 80 feet, by hand, to hit water!!!!!!!

It was a month or so ago that my missionary friend contacted me and said the well project might actually be accepted if we had financing for 3 wells in the same region! At the same time, another Board member submitted a proposal named "Water4Life"which was accepted by the Janus Project, affiliated with the Ironman race to be held in Hawaii in late 2008. If the goal is reached, and is in the top fund raisers, Janus awards substantial monetary awards!!!! And many villages will have "Water4Life".

How did this chapter make it into the book? This is not a "done deal" (Not yet visible anyway). It is here because it is obvious the Holy Spirit has touched the hearts and spirits of some believers who realize there are times when God desires to meet physical needs to give credibility to the gospel message about a Savior who loves them and died for them!

It just may be that by the time you are reading this book there will be an update on our web site telling how much was raised and how many wells can be drilled!

You see, ***THIS MIRACLE REALLY IS NOT ABOUT MONEY.*** It is about God moving in the hearts and lives of His children to meet needs half a world away!

GOD AWARENESS: Many years ago, precious friends of mine, a pastor and his wife, came to Burkina to help us share the love of Christ among the Dagara. When we arrived at the house, I was sharing with them some of the "house rules". Among them were the rules of shower and bathroom procedures dealing with the safeguarding of what little water we had. I had a cement water trough in the back and needed water brought in with barrels and pumped into a holding tank above and beside the house. Without going into details, let me just say we had a system of using small pebbles which would indicate at what point we were allowed to flush the toilet! This was all normal and routine for me. It was not that way for them! They were such good sports! Before they left Burkina and headed home, my friend Marcia told me she would never, ever again complain about their monthly water bill!

The only source of alleviating the heat was a small six to eight inch fan which was attached by cord and paperclip to a car battery. Once again we needed to ration the use as we had no way at the house to re-charge the batteries when they ran down. We also needed to be very frugal about opening the refrigerator as electricity ran only a few hours daily and once the cool air escaped...that was the end of cool water. Marcia never said it, but they may not complain about the electric bill either!

Beloved, most of those reading this book live in America. You live in homes with air conditioning or at least fans. When clothes need washing you wash them with little or no thought about water. When you shower, little or no thought is given to the length of the shower. Lawns are watered to keep grass and flowers pretty and alive. Hoses are used full force to wash our cars. Outings are planned and held at the lake or the beach. Water. In your homes. Water. For your yards. Water. For your entertainment. Water.

In the space given please record your thoughts about this chapter. Are you a good guardian of natural resources? Can you think of some do-able ways to conserve energy? Ways to conserve water? _____

_____

_____

_____

_____

_____

_____

_____

_____

Let's Pray: "Lord Jesus. You know far better than we that water is the source of life! Our bodies need water. Our bodies are comprised of it. You know how many people in this world are dying of diseases caused by drinking and bathing in contaminated water. And Lord Jesus, You know how many people in the world still wait to receive the Living Water! You know how many are thirsting to know the Water Giver. Help us Lord…to take the message of the Living Water to a thirsty and dry world! In Jesus' Name. Amen."

** For as update on this God Story, go to our website, www. shatteringdarkness.org and the link Water4Life!!!!!

** Be sure to see one of our well pictures located in the Photo Gallery Section**

HIS TIME. HIS WORD.

～♉ ♉～

"For as the rain and the snow come down from
heaven, And do not return without watering
the earth And making it bear and sprout, And
furnishing seed to the sower and bread to the
eater; So will My word be which goes forth
from My mouth; It will not return to Me empty,
Without accomplishing what I desire, And without
succeeding in the matter for which I sent it."
Isaiah 55:11-12

"The grass withers, and the flower fades, but the
Word of our God stands forever." Isaiah 40:8

For more than five years we had used one primary
translation of the French Bible. We used it for writing
our village lessons. We used it for writing all of our radio
programs. We used it in all of our churches. We used it for
Bible Studies. The version is "Francais Courant", an equivalent to the English New International Version.

We found it much easier to teach, and new believers
or new "readers" found it much easier to understand than
the "Louis Seconde" which is equivalent to the King James
Version. And then we could not find the version anywhere!
We went to a Bible book store. They said they no longer

were being produced! We called another bookstore and were told the same thing.

What were we to do? All of our work since 2000! Impossible to re-write everything! How does one replace the hundreds of Bibles we had already distributed?? How can a Bible translation just "stop" being produced?????? We prayed. We kept asking people if they knew people who might have a source in a neighboring country that would still have some of these Bibles available.

One afternoon, a deacon in an Assembly of God church was at the house. I mentioned the problem and asked if he knew of any source or any possible contact. A few days later he stopped by the house to say he had made some calls and gotten counsel and had located one or possibly two cartons (40 Bibles to a carton) in Bobo (our second largest city here in Burkina). Oh! How marvelous!

One tiny problem however...how was I going to pay for 1-2 cartons of Bibles????

"Daniel, please call your friend and say I want all the Bibles they have. That will be somewhere between 40 and 80. I want them all. We may never be able to find them again." At the same moment I was asking him to purchase all of them, I was thinking: "Well, Lord, what will I *not pay* this month so we can purchase Your Holy Word? I know this is a necessity. Nothing we do is more important than getting Your Word into the hands and hearts of the people."

I asked Daniel to stop by the house the next morning before his scheduled trip to Bobo and I would give him the money for the Bibles.

That same evening...an email arrived from our Shattering Darkness Treasurer advising me that a former missionary to Burkina Faso now residing in the United States had sent a check in the amount of $1,000.00 to be used wherever needed!

Wherever needed!? Beloved...*THIS MIRACLE IS NOT ABOUT MONEY!* This *Miracle* is about a family in America praying for and believing in what the Lord is doing through Shattering Darkness Ministries. It is about a one income home with two teen-aged daughters (one in college) with a continuing desire to seek to glorify God in their serving and giving.

The *Miracle* is about the Timing of our God. *Before* I knew Bibles had been located in Burkina. *Before* I asked Daniel to purchase the Bibles. *Before* I knew how we would pay for the Bibles...the Holy Spirit of the living God had already acted upon the hearts of a husband and his family. The check already mailed. The check already received. The email already sent!!!!!!!

God's Word. God's Time. God's Story. His Glory!

GOD AWARENESS: Our people in Burkina Faso love the Word of God. Those who can read devour it! They feast upon its truths and teachings. No matter where they are or what they are doing...open their backpacks and you will find a Bible! There is no Bible in their ethnic language so we use the French Bible, as French is the national language in Burkina Faso. We take so much for granted here in the U. S. Bibles come in all shapes, sizes and types of translations. All colors of the rainbow. We have a plethora of study and research helps. Do we use them? Do we, you and I, feast upon the Holy Word??

I am going to ask you to do something very specific. I want you to go through your house and gather up all unused Bibles. You know the ones I mean. The ones gathering dust. The ones you no longer use. The ones on display. The ones on shelves and desks and in drawers. Gather them all. Place them all in one spot.

Now, I want you to pray and ask the Lord to reveal the people in your life that need a Bible. This may be family members or friends. This may be co-workers. This may be parents or children. This may be a neighbor. Once the Lord reveals the people to you, I want you to begin praying for them. Ask that they be receptive to this gift-giving. I want you to pray and ask God to show you when the people will be ready to receive the Bible. And now, present to them the Holy Word of God!

To whom did you give the Bibles? Were they receptive? What did they say? How did they react? Were you nervous?

_____

_____

_____

_____

Have you ever done anything like this before?

_____

_____

_____

_____

How long did you pray before giving the Bibles?

_____

_____

_____

_____

How many Bibles did you find as you gathered them in your home?_____

If you did not have any Bibles to give away I want to present a challenge to you. I want you to go to a Bible book store. I want you to choose a Bible in an easy to read and understand version. Then I want you to purchase the Bible and present it to someone you care about and who needs the Word of God.

Let's Pray: "Oh Father God! Lead me to a place of being passionate about Your Holy Word! Please birth in me a desire to feast upon it! Please do such a work in me that I will die of thirst and hunger if I do not eat and drink of the fountain of Your eternal Word! Help me to love Your Word as You do! Help me to pray it back to You! Help me to hide it in my heart! Help me to feed it to others. Help me, Lord. Help us. In the Name above all Names, the Name of our Jesus we pray. Amen."

** Be sure to look at the Bible in our Photo Gallery found at the end of this book**

MIRACLE MANNA

❧ ❧

"If I were hungry, I would not tell you; For the world is Mine, and all it contains...Offer to God a sacrifice of thanksgiving, and pay your vows to the Most High; And call upon Me in the day of trouble; I shall rescue you, and you will honor Me." Psalm 50:12, 14-15

The fall of 2007 found me quite often in specific prayer for our ministry. Funds were not being received. Some pledges were not kept. I was desperate before the Lord. I did not let Patrice, the Director of Ministry and Missions (attending seminary in a different country at the time) know of the desperate situation. We also had three couples being trained in Bible School at the same time. The training was vital for the continued strength and growth of Shattering Darkness Ministries in the years to come. I knew if I told Patrice how desperate things were, he would leave seminary!

Day and night I would cry out to God. I did not understand. I knew Shattering Darkness was birthed in the heart of God. It was His ministry, not mine. I had a good deal of respect for those who had made substantial pledges. Yet no number of phone calls, emails, and letters prompted any response of any kind.

Perhaps some of you are like me...when stressed....
clean something!!
So early one morning I cleaned out a small cabinet in
my bedroom where I keep my clothes. I asked my guard to
take it outside and give it a fresh coat of paint. I threw all the
clothes and a tiny spiral notebook on the bed.

Later that evening I replaced all the clothes but saw the
tiny notebook on the far side of the bed snuggled into the
corner of the headboard-bookcase. I left it and figured I
would retrieve it the next morning. After all, I had not even
opened it in more than two years, nothing of importance
could be written or placed inside.

I tossed and turned on top of the bedspread throughout
the night. Early before sunrise I turned toward the far side
of the bed and my hand fell on something "slick". Believe
me when I tell you, that there is no missionary anywhere in
the world that wants their hand on something unknown in
the blackness of night or early morning. Did I really want to
open my eyes to see what I was touching?? (At least whatever it was had not moved!) I slowly opened my eyes. What
I saw was a brand new two dollar Burkina bill! "Where did
this come from? How did this get here? We have not had
"new" money here since the change in currency nearly three
years ago!"

I sat up. I saw a few more bills on top of the cover. "What
is this?" I turned down the spread and what did I see?????
BRAND NEW $2.00 BILLS FROM HEAD TO FOOT!

"OK Lord...what are You telling me? What is this all
about?" A tender voice responded to my heart: "I am telling
you that I have heard your cry. I know your need. And I will
be abundant toward you."

I sat stunned. Tears filled my eyes.

I gathered all the money and counted the bills. Seventy
(70) in all! An equivalent of $350.00 American dollars!

A few months later we gave a special "love" offering at the dedication of our then new church/training center dual building. The Lord made it clear I was to place the Miracle Manna in the offering which was going toward the construction of four new worship/prayer buildings in four of our villages. I am grateful the Lord allowed me to keep one of the bills which I have laminated and have in my Bible! I do not ever want to forget.

THIS MIRACLE HAD NOTHING TO DO WITH MONEY. The miracle was God responding to the need of one of His own to know He was near to them and aware of their needs. This miracle had to do with the assurance of provision, awareness and presence. This miracle had to do with a very personal intervention of God in the life of one who needed a personal touch from her Savior.

GOD AWARENESS: I want to encourage you to be honest with God. What are your needs? What are your legitimate needs... realizing that our needs are very different than our wants. Search your heart. Is mismanagement of money a concern? If so, repent and ask God to show you how to get out of debt. Is selfishness or extravagance a problem? If so, repent and ask God to change your heart. Is the economy or a growing family or being a single mom the issue? Have you turned to God in your desperation?

Write your honest feelings to these questions here.

_____
_____
_____
_____
_____
_____
_____
_____

_____

_____
_____
_____
_____
_____
_____
_____
_____
_____
_____
_____
_____

Now I want you to pray and ask God to show you some tangible ways to turn your financial distress around. Note them below. (Example: destroy all credit cards, ask your church to recommend a financial consultant, attend "Crown Ministries" meetings if offered at your church or a nearby church, begin eating at home rather than in restaurants and drive-throughs.)

_____
_____
_____
_____
_____
_____
_____
_____
_____
_____
_____
_____

_____

_____

_____

_____

_____.

Let's pray: "Lord Jesus, the One who created and owns the world, we are here before You because we need You. We need Your counsel. We need Your wisdom. We need Your encouragement. Lord, in a world and economy shouting to us, "Buy it! Charge it! Upgrade it! Change it! You are worth it!", You speak to us of financial management, caution, trust and Your provision. Lord, please forgive us our extravagancies and teach us to live in a way which allows us to honor You in our money management and in our giving! In Jesus' Name we pray. Amen."

** Be sure to see the dollar bill the Lord allowed me to keep as a souvenir of His divine touch on my life at a very emotional and needy time in my walk with Him. It is found in our Photo Gallery section at the end of this book.**

KEEPER OF HIS PROMISES

᭲᭲

"Because of the proof given by this ministry they will glorify God for your obedience to your confession of the gospel of Christ, and for the liberality of your contribution to them and to all...Thanks be to God for His indescribable gift." 2 Corinthians 10:13,15

This chapter will be the most difficult to write because it is so very personal. In early 2008, the Lord spoke to my heart saying He wanted me to pray and fast for forty days. I sensed that this was a result of my desperation and crying out to Him to provide for Shattering Darkness Ministries. I was dedicating from 4AM to 4PM daily for forty days to pray about faith partners, our Board of Directors, vision and future ministry expansion.

Day number one, I was up, awake and ready to pray for our ministry. God had something different in mind. He began to show me areas in my life that were displeasing to Him! He showed me areas where I was not honoring Him! He showed me areas needing to be confessed and strongholds needing to be broken! This continued, through my tears and broken-heartedness and shame for three full days! Three days of weeping and repenting. Three days of God drying my tears and pardoning my sin. Three days while God created in me a clean heart and a renewed spirit. Three days while God brought me to a new and deep place with Him. Three days of a suffering and pain that was new to me. Three days for God to get me to a place where I could approach Him with a new passion and a new heart.

I journaled during those forty days and you are now ready to get a glimpse of those days. "Now get on your knees and ask Me" the Lord spoke to my heart. After three days of cleansing and purging me, He was now ready to listen to my requests for our ministry.

"Lord, I would really like us to receive $16,000 so we can pay off all our land taxes and the ministry site will be debt free."

"Your faith is too small" the Holy Spirit responded.

"Lord, I am not finished yet! I also want $8,000.00 so we can build a place for our youth to come to study as well as a place to hang out which will keep them out of the bars and the bedrooms."

"Your faith is too small" was the Lord's response once again. And I seemed to sense that He was disappointed.

"OK."

Deep breath. Very deep breath. Eyes lifted to heaven. Heart pounding. "Lord, we need 1 million dollars so this ministry will have a solid foundation and no longer be a day to day or month to month financial challenge." And then I waited. I waited for the Lord to chuckle. I waited for Him to correct me for being arrogant or foolish or selfish. I waited for Him to respond. "That is more like it. You are now beginning to understand." Whoa! A million dollars? Really? "Lord, really?"

Very early the following morning, long before the 4 A.M. alarm, I was awake. The moment I awoke, before opening my eyes, before washing my face or brushing my teeth, I began, "OK Lord. Now, who do I know that has money? And who do they know that has money? And…."

"Stop it! Just stop it! Get your mind and motives off things that I am responsible for! I am already working. Just Let Me be God. That is Who I am."

Well, now, you are thinking...hmmm, that was pretty clear! Well, sometimes I do not know when to let things be. And in spite of my age sometimes I still pout! So I pouted. I pouted and asked, "Lord, then what is my role in this? What am I to do in all this?"

"You are to keep praying. You are to keep believing. You are to keep trusting. Let Me be God. That is Who I am."

Nearly nine months have passed since my 4 to 4 for 40 pilgrimage. We have not yet received a donation or multiple donations equaling a million dollars! The other evening I had dinner with one of our Faith Partners. She and I were discussing some things and she shared a time in her life that she needed a car and had no money. The Lord told her to thank Him for the car. She had no money to buy one. She had no source to borrow from. Yet the Lord told her then and there to thank Him. As she spoke those words the Lord spoke to my heart. "Thank Me" He said. "Thank Me for the Miracle that is not yet visible. Have the faith to thank Me." That conversation occurred two months ago. Since that time I have been thanking God for His provision. I have been thanking Him for the answer He has already given. I will keep on thanking Him. I will keep on praying. I will keep on trusting. I will keep on believing. And I wait.

GOD AWARENESS: Beloved, our Lord created the world. All belongs to Him. Let us begin today to be aware of His presence and His power and His love and His promise. Let us be faithful in thanking Him! Let us become believers who walk by faith and not by sight. Believers who walk by faith and not reason or logic. Believers who walk by faith and not finances. Let us glory in Him as we praise, exalt and believe! I want you to look at Psalm 50 verses 10 through 15.

Meditate upon them. Now I want you to record in the space
provided some of your thoughts.

_____

_____

_____

_____

_____

_____

_____

    I hope that among other things you noted from verse ten
that the world and all in it belongs to God! I hope as well that
you found comfort and encouragement from verse eleven as
you realized that God knows where you are and knows all
that you are experiencing in these days. In verses twelve and
thirteen I hope you realized afresh and anew that God is in
total control and has no "need" of material things from us. In
verse fourteen we discovered what the Lord does desire from
us...our faithfulness and our praise and thanksgiving. (He
wants us to be aware of His presence every moment of every
day.) It is my heart's desire that you realized in verse fifteen
that the Lord loves it when we pray and when we bring our
needs to Him. He promises as well to rescue us. "**And you
will honor Me.**" Beloved...it is not about us. It never has
been. It is all about Jesus. It always has been. Maybe we just
lost sight of that for a while!

    Let's Pray: "Lord Jesus, worthy art Thou who was slain
to receive power and riches and wisdom and might and glory
and blessing, for You and You alone shed Your blood and by
it, purchased for God people from every tribe and tongue
and people and nation! You purchased me, glorious Savior!
Me! I am no longer my own. I have been bought with a price.
Your precious blood! Lord Jesus, make me a servant who
carries Your Word and truth to a lost world. Please make

me a handmaiden who tells Your Story, Lord Jesus. A God Story. Amen"

HOW DID I GET THERE
FROM HERE?

৩৯ ৯৯

"He was despised and forsaken of men, A man of
sorrows, and acquainted with grief; And like one
from whom men hide their face, He was despised,
and we did not esteem Him. Surely our griefs He
Himself bore, And our sorrows He carried; Yet
we ourselves esteemed Him stricken, Smitten of
God, and afflicted. But He was pierced through
for our transgressions, He was crushed for our
iniquities; The chastening for our well-being fell
upon Him, and by His scourging we are healed."
Isaiah 53:3-5

It smells like smoke! In fact it smells like something is
burning! I look. Then I quickly look away! Yet something keeps drawing me back to this horrible scene! It is
as though I am a part of this drama yet at the same time
withdrawn from it. I see an arm. It is reaching deep into the
cavern of flames and destruction! I want to scream out, "NO!
NO! Do not reach down into that pit! You will be hurt! You
will die! My mouth does not open. My lips remain pressed
together. Yet the Rescuer looks toward me as He simultane-
ously removes His arm from the burning inferno. His arm

is scorched as I knew it would be. There is pain on His face and I hear it in His sigh. But wait! There is something in His injured hand! What?? Oh! It can not possibly be! Impossible to remain afar off, I draw closer and closer to see what has been rescued. But...how... I can see it all clearly now. *I am in His hand*!!! His injured hand! His scorched hand! *This Rescuer, my Rescuer, has reached into the very pit of hell in order to save me!*

"Forgive me, Lord Jesus! I see it all now. I was dead in my trespasses and sin. The evil one had captured me and I was bound to an eternity in his domain! Yet You were driven by Your love for me, You would not allow me to be condemned! Forgive me, Lord, forgive me!"

Many people through the years have asked how I ended up on the mission field, and beyond even that, how I ended up in Burkina Faso! What follows is my story.

I came to know Jesus as my personal Savior at the age of twenty-nine. I was married at the age of thirty and widowed at the age of thirty-five. Within a few months I was in Indonesia on a short-term Impact trip. It was then I realized God's call upon my life was international missions! I knew that the Lord was giving me the privilege to be His ambassador in foreign lands among the nations and peoples who, like I had been, were enslaved to sin and its penalty.

In the next ten years I served on staff at two marvelous churches. I also returned to school and earned a Bachelor's degree in Religious Education and a Master's degree in Divinity. A year of language school in France followed as well. During this total of eleven years, my prayer remained the same. "Lord, please send me somewhere that no one has ever been. Send me where others will not go, whether because of danger or difficult conditions. Please send me to a place needing to know of You."

I added to my heart's cry in 1998 as my prayer then became, "Lord, please release me to go to a place where I will be free to see new visions and to dream new dreams. Please send me to a place where whatever amount of time I have left will impact eternity. Please send me to a place where people are ready to hear of You. *Because I am too old. Because Time is too short. Because People are too lost. Because Hell is too real."*

The Lord heard and answered "Yes" to my pleas. Ministry among the Dagara people group began in 1998.

The Lord continued to prune me and change me. In 2002 I sensed a change was coming. My spirit was restless. My heart was heavy. Problems were surfacing with members of my American ministry team members. So much that caused me pain then I now realize were all a part of God's Master Plan in my life!

The apostle Paul and his friend Barnabas desired people to be saved and churches planted and new believers to grow in faith. Yet their vision as to how those goals would be achieved, and the personnel who would be entrusted the task differed greatly. These two Christian ministers separated and went different ways. But history shows us that the ministry was not diminished! It grew! It expanded!

In 2004 I resigned from the mission agency which had commissioned me to Burkina Faso. But it was, and continues to be, God who sent me and keeps me in Burkina Faso, West Africa. Thus, in the fall of 2004, Shattering Darkness was inaugurated. She had been birthed in the heart of God since eternity!

God gave me the name "Shattering Darkness" in the summer of 2004 when I went stateside in order to establish the ministry, complete the incorporation papers, and enlist a Board of Directors. I was sitting at the table in a mission home in Clermont, Florida. I was talking with the Lord and asked Him what our name was. (This is important information the attorney needs before papers can be filed!) The Lord spoke to my heart and asked me in turn "What have I called you to do? What is your task in West Africa?" I pondered and reflected and then said, "You have entrusted me with the task of shattering spiritual darkness with the Light of Christ." Once again I sensed the Spirit of God speaking to my spirit as He replied, "Exactly." A few hours later I was reading Isaiah. Chapter 9 verse 2 says: *"The people who walk in darkness Will see a great light; Those who live in a dark land, The light will shine on them."*

WOW! Moments later the Lord drew me to the book of Acts, chapter 26 and I was looking at the apostle Paul sharing his conversion testimony in verses 16-18.

"But arise, and stand on your feet; for this purpose I have appeared to you, to appoint you a minister and a witness not only to the things which you have seen, but also to the things in which I will appear to you: delivering you from the Jewish people and from the Gentiles, to whom I am sending you, to open their eyes so that they may turn from darkness to light and from the dominion of satan to God, in order that they may receive forgiveness of sins and an inheritance among those who have been sanctified by faith in Me."

In His graciousness and mercy, the Lord used His Holy Word to confirm the ministry, the task and the name for Shattering Darkness Ministries!

GOD AWARENESS: I would like you to close your eyes a moment. I would like you to re-live the moment when you gave your life to Christ. Were you a child? Were you a teen-ager? Were you in your twenties, thirties, or forty-something? Were you alone? Were you at a youth camp or sitting in church? In the spaces provided below record some of what you remember of the time in your life that you became a Christian.

Some of you may have never thought about this before. You may never have needed to write out your conversion, your salvation, testimony. Perhaps some of you are not sure of your relationship with the Lord Jesus.

Are you not sure? Are you finding yourself thinking, 'I hope I am a Christian,' ' I think I am a Christian,' ' I am not sure, I do not know.' Do not be embarrassed. Many people are thinking the same things.

One of the reasons for writing this book is to help people be sure of their relationship with the Lord Jesus. I am not speaking of 'religion.' I am not speaking of 'denominations.' Not a church. Not a denomination. Not a relative. Not a pastor, priest or rabbi. It is only by having a personal relationship with Jesus, gained by repentance of sin and acceptance in faith, are we assured of heaven. In the space provided here record any questions you have. Make note of things you are not sure about.

_____

_____

_____

_____

_____

_____

_____

_____

_____

_____

Think on this a while as we continue on to the next chapter. At the conclusion, you will have the opportunity to pray and be sure you are His!!

Let's Pray: "Lord Jesus, please teach me to recognize Your activity in my life. Please help me to recognize Your voice. Please help me to trust You, to follow You and to obey You. Please make me brave and bold enough to listen! I do not want to be afraid or hesitant toward Your actions in my life. Please make my heart and soul and spirit be open and alive to Your activity in my life. Help me to be thankful. In Jesus' Name I ask this, Amen"

You can look at our website to get just a glimpse of what the Lord has done since 2004. www.shatteringdarkness.org is our website address.

CONCLUSION

"Praise the Lord! I will give thanks to the Lord
with all my heart,
In the company of the upright and in the
assembly.
Great are the works of the Lord;
They are studied by all who delight in them.
Splendid and majestic is His work;
And His righteousness endures forever.
He has made His wonders to be remembered;
The Lord is gracious and compassionate." Psalm
111: 1-4

A WORD FROM THE AUTHOR

᠊ᡕᡘ ᡘᡕ᠊

I began this book by thanking the Miracle Worker Who was willing to save someone like me. He waited for me. He drew me to Himself time and time again. And each time, I said, "NO". But the loving Lord would not allow the world nor satan to keep me! There are still times when I can actually see the Lord reaching His hand down into the fires of hell in order to rescue me! As He lifts His hand with me safe in it, I see how scorched they are from the fire!

Perhaps some of you reading this book are wondering how to find my Miracle-Working and Seeker-of-lost-souls God. Perhaps there are others who have been refreshed and reminded anew of the depth and expanse of our Savior's love toward those who believe! My heart's desire is that all of us have been changed and invigorated as we interacted with the Light of the World!

For any who have read this book and are doubting your relationship with Jesus, there is no better time than this very moment to seal your eternity with Him! He is waiting to receive you. He is ready to forgive you. His arms are opened wide. His heart is yearning for you.

Can you recall a time when the Lord used Scripture to affirm a choice or decision you made? Can you recall the time the Lord drew you to Himself and you repented of sin? Are you not sure? Have you caught yourself wondering about your personal relationship with Jesus as you have read this book? Have the glimpses of Jesus caught you unawares, or jealous or wondering why nothing like this has even happened to you? Beloved....you are loved of God. He sent His only begotten Son to suffer and die on a Cross so that you might find eternal life! The blood of Jesus is powerful and holy enough to cleanse you of all sin! Please...do not put this book down without being sure of your relationship with the living Christ!

I want you to do something for me; no, *I want you to do something for you*! I want you to look at the prayer that follows. Then, if it expresses the desire of your heart and soul, I want you to pray the prayer aloud. Offer it to the One Who died to set you free!

Let's Pray: "Holy Jesus, I admit to You and to myself, I am a sinner. I am separated from You because of my sin, my rebellion. I come to You now, and by faith ask You, Lord Jesus, to cleanse me of my sin. Please wash me in the blood You shed on Calvary. Please fill me with Your Holy Spirit to guide me and to help me grow in faith. Please help me to honor You in and through my life from this moment forward. I receive Your forgiveness by faith and thank You. In Jesus' Name I pray. Amen."

Did you pray this prayer? If you prayed with a repentant heart, God heard you and has forgiven you, He has saved you!

Are you wondering what to do now? Good question!

1.) Tell someone of your decision to follow Jesus.
2.) Find a Bible teaching church and join it.
3.) Be faithful in church and a Bible Study class.
4.) Pray each day.
5.) Read your Bible each day.

6.) Cultivate friendships with faithful followers of Jesus.

If you do not have a Bible, contact our ministry and we will suggest a good Bible translation for you to use. If you are not currently attending church, we will also aide you in connecting with a good Bible-believing fellowship in your city. Please allow us the privilege of rejoicing with you at your decision to place your life in the hands of Jesus!

Contact information is available on our web site at www. shatteringdarkness.org

PHOTO GALLERY

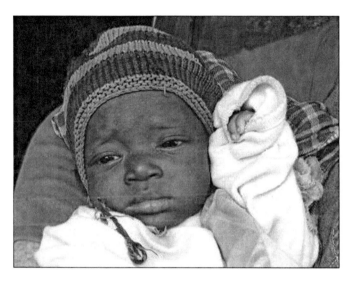

Praise the Lord Lynn, and forge
benefits – who forgives all your
heals all your diseases, who rec...
life from the pit and crowns you with
and compassion.   Ps 10...
        I am the God that healeth T...
            Jehovah-Rapha

SHATTERING DARKNESS
SONG LYRICS

Lyrics to: *YOU TAKE MY BREATH AWAY*

You spoke and the world came into being. You breathed the breath of life into a man.
And the thought of You, the very thought of YOU.... takes my breath away!
YOU came and walked upon the very earth that YOU had made.
YOU laughed and YOU cried. YOU healed and YOU fed. You warned and YOU called.
The sins of man YOU forgave!
And Lord, the thought of YOU, the very thought of YOU....takes my breath away.

YOU called my name and waited. Time and time again. Refusing to let go.
Refusing to take "NO". Not wanting hell and judgment my end.
A perfect plan You have in place for all who repent and believe.
No matter the sin and no matter the when Your Holy Blood to cleanse!
Your Holy Spirit to abide. Your Holy Word to instruct. Your Holy Promise never to leave.
And the thought of You, the very thought of YOU...takes my breath away!

I gaze now, Lord, upon Thy face and marvel at Thy boundless grace!
And the thought of YOU, the very thought of YOU... takes my breath away!
Prophet, Priest and King, Lamb of God, Creator of all things,
the Great I AM, Adonai, One True God, Giver of good things.

Savior, Master, Eternal God.....
YOU take my breath away!!!!!

One day soon YOU will come again gathering Your
   bride.
All suffering to cease. All promises to keep. Forever and
   always with YOU to abide.
And the thought of YOU, the very thought of YOU...
   takes my breath away!

(The rest very slow, almost a whisper)

Lord Jesus... YOU take my breath away!
King Jesus...YOU take my breath away.
Precious Jesus...YOU take my breath away.
My Jesus...YOU take my breath away
Jesus..........

Lyrics to: *WHO PRAYS FOR ME?*

When I find myself all alone
Whether in a crowd
Or no one near
Who prays for me?

"Christ Jesus is the One Who died, but even more has been
raised;
He is also at the right hand of God and intercedes for us"
(Rom 8:34)

When my health
Or my heart, my home
Or my spirit fails
Who prays for me?

"Therefore He (Jesus) is always able to save those who
come to God through Him,
since He always lives to intercede for them." (Hebrews
7:25)

When I stumble or fall
Or walk straight into sin
Ashamed and forsaken
Bearing the penalty within
Who prays for me?

"I have prayed for you that your faith may not fail.
And you, when you have turned back, strengthen your
brothers" (Luke 22:32)

Dear friend
When you find yourself all alone
Whether in a crowd

Or no one near
Who prays for you?

When your health
Or your heart, your home
Or your spirit fails
Who prays for you?

When you stumble or fall
Or walk straight into sin
Ashamed and forsaken
Bearing the penalty within
Who prays for you?
When so very far from loved ones
So very weak in battle
So very frail in body
Who prays for me?

"The Holy Spirit joins to help in our weakness,
because we do not know what to pray for as we should,
But the Holy Spirit intercedes for us with unspoken
    groaning." Rom 8: 26

Jesus! The Savior. Creator. Forgiver. Strengthener.
    Confidant. Pardoner.
The One Whose blood cleanses us of all sin. The One Who
    loves you.
The One Who is waiting is the One Who is praying for you!
    For me.
For us!

Lyrics to: *THERE IS ONLY ONE*

There is only one Way to be forgiven of sin. There is only one way to enter within. There is only one Way to find oneness with God. And only one way on heaven's terrain to trod.

There is only one Way. His Name is Jesus.

There is only one Savior; no matter your race.. There is only one Savior no matter your place. There is only one Savior no matter your opinion. There is only one Savior for one..or for millions.

There is only one Savior. His Name is Jesus.

There is only one Name under heaven given. There is only one Name to call upon to be forgiven. There is only one Name at which all knees will bow. There is only one Name all believers avow.

There is only one Name. His Name is Jesus.

There is only one Road which leads us to glory. There is only one Truth: the "Good News" story. There is only one Master, Savior and King. There is only one Lord to whom the angels sing!

There is only one Road. His name is Jesus.

There is only one Bible, translations aside. It tells of the Savior for our sins crucified!
There is only one Truth as the Bible instructs us. There is only one Hope..the One Who died and rose again for us!

There is only one Living Word. His Name is Jesus.

There is only One Who for us intercedes. There is only One Who to His Father He pleads. There is only One Who promised His Holy Spirit. There is only One Who empowers us to believe it!

There is only One Who is our Mediator. His Name is Jesus.

There is only one Hope. There is only one Way. There is only one Redeemer to show us the way. There is only one Savior and only one Lord. There is only one Jesus, no matter the lies of the world. He loves you so much. His very life for you He gave. He asks not for your money. He asks not for good works. He asks not for your religion, nor for your excuses. He desires your heart. There is only One. His Name is Jesus. His Name is Jesus.

Lyrics to: *IT WAS YOU*

Based on Psalm 74:12-17 Read the verses before singing

IT WAS YOU FROM THE BEGINNING
IT WAS YOU Who sought out Moses and Abraham and Gideon.
IT WAS YOU Who waited for their obedience and their loyalty.
IT WAS YOU Who called to Samuel and Daniel..honored each time they obeyed.
IT WAS YOU Who watched over Joseph and
IT WAS YOU Who gave courage to Rahab.
IT WAS YOU.

Old Testament heroes. We know their stories by heart. Indeed they suffered. Indeed they believed.
Indeed they knew You in part. Oh, but today we have more knowledge. And oh, today more stories to tell.
Today more pictures to post. And today more media hi-tech. Yet..Today.. do we still only know YOU in part??

IT WAS YOU Who came to call sinners.
IT WAS YOU Who died for their sins.
IT WAS YOU Who rose to life on the third day.....death never more again to win!
IT WAS YOU Who conquered death, sin, satan and the grave
IT WAS YOU Who called. Stephen. Paul. Matthew. Luke. Timothy...and people like me.
IT WAS YOU Who waited. Excuses given. Lies told. Lives in disgrace and dishonor. Alcohol. Drugs. Abortion. Divorce. Rebellion.
IT WAS YOU Who forgave. ALL!
IT WAS YOU Who loved first. So that we could love You.

New Testament people. Just like you and me.
(Begin here VERY FAST AND FRENZIED…lots of drums and pounding music as though driving us faster and faster to destruction)
Far from God. Running. Hiding. Faster….Faster….. Faster…..Another drink….
Another drink….More cigarettes…..More drugs…..More porn…..more money…..
More More More More…
STOP ALL SOUNDS AND MUSIC HERE
IT WAS YOU…Jesus.
Ready and wanting to forgive. Seeking the lost. Loving them. Calling them. Giving renewal and pardon. Creating new hearts.
IT WAS YOU.
IT ALWAYS WAS.
AND STILL IS!
Very quiet..very mellow….IT WAS YOU. IT WAS YOU. AND STILL IS.

Printed in the United States
216620BV00001B/2/P

9 781607 912262